Brigid

Brigid

HISTORY, MYSTERY, AND MAGICK
OF THE CELTIC GODDESS

Courtney Weber

WEISER BOOKS
San Francisco, CA / Newburyport, MA

This edition first published in 2015 by Weiser Books, an imprint of

Red Wheel/Weiser, LLC
With offices at:
665 Third Street, Suite 400
San Francisco, CA 94107
www.redwheelweiser.com

ISBN: 978-1-57863-567-2

Library of Congress Cataloging-in-Publication Data available upon request.

Cover design by Jim Warner.
Cover photograph: A Muse, 1895 (oil on slate), Point, Armand (1861–1932) / Private Collection / Photo © Christie's Images / Bridgeman Images
Interior by Maureen Forys, Happenstance Type-O-Rama
Typeset in Kepler and Benton Sans

Printed in the United States of America
EBM

10 9 8 7 6 5 4 3 2 1

Contents

Dedication

For Donn Kean and Zan "Puck" Fraser: Scribes in this world, Muses in the next. You are missed.

And of course, for Brid.

CHAPTER 1

Who Is Brigid?

Brigid, that is, the female poet, daughter of the Dagda. This is Brigit the female seer, or woman of insight, i.e., the goddess whom poets used to worship, for her cult was very great and very splendid. It is for this reason that they call her the goddess of poets by this title, and her sisters were Brigid the woman of leechcraft and Brigit, the woman of smithcraft, i.e., goddesses, i.e., three daughters of the Dagda are they. By their names the goddess Brigid was called by all the Irish.

—CORMAC MAC CUILENNÁIN, Tenth-century scholar

A character quaint and fierce, powerful yet graceful, has woven a trail across oceans and borders, cultures and languages, practices, folklore, prayer, and song, creating a strangely perfect sort of unity melded only under a divine hammer. She stands watch over the delicate, serene trickle of Ireland's holy wells and stoic Welsh cathedrals. She appears in Glastonbury's healing temples, depicted with flaming sun-hair, and also in murals of the Haitian Voudon Lwa, with a pale face in a wild, clashing costume, watching over the cemetery. She stands with a shepherd's staff over a tiny fox as the patron saint of New York City's Loisaida. In Ireland, she has been called Bhríde, Brig-eoit,

Brigit. In Scotland, Brigh, Bridi, Bridean, Brüd. Wales has called her Bregit, Breit, Breid, Freit, Ffraid, Ffred, Fride. In what is now France she has been called Brigette or Britta, and in England, she was known as Brigitae or Brigantia. This is the Goddess of the forge and anvil, of poets, painters, and prophets. She is a Goddess of healing as well as battle, of fire but also water, of love and of death. She blesses small animals, guards orphaned children, and challenges authority. She has crossed the chasm of regional land Goddess to Christian saint and back again to a contemporary Goddess of a global scope. Distinct as the multitude of tongues that speak her name, and deeply rooted in creation, destruction, regeneration, and sometimes contradiction—this is Brigid.

A teacher of mine believes a whole spiritual tradition could be filled solely with Brigid devotees. In the Neo-Pagan community, I have seen a plethora of covens dedicated to her and met more Brigid devotees than I can count. This does not include the hundreds of churches, women's groups, convents, and other spiritual or secular charity organizations dedicated to Brigid. She is everywhere and she is not relegated to one faith.

But who is Brigid? So much about her remains a mystery. How did a Goddess whose origins lay in the soils and waters of the Celtic world slowly but deftly take hold in so many places, both at the source and thousands of miles away? How did she begin and, perhaps more curiously, what has she become?

BRIGID THE EXALTED: A CELTIC GODDESS

To understand a Deity, one must attempt to understand the history and nature of the first people to worship that Deity. Brigid originated in the pantheon of the Celtic people—the residents of Ireland and the British Isles. Much like Brigid, the history of these people is mysterious and complex. I once heard a description that exploring the Celts' historic identity is like watching television with the sound off. One can kind of decipher what's going on, but quite a bit of the story is lost. Mysterious artifacts tell us a bit about what the ancient Celts were like, but prior to the introduction of Christianity, the Celts left no written records. We are left guessing at what these pieces meant to the people who utilized them. Neighbors of the ancient Celts left the most descriptive accounts, but this is a little problematic. Most of the history written about the ancient Celts was penned by foreigners or enemies who may not have had an adequate understanding of Celtic culture or who likely wrote slanted accounts. Sometimes, Deities and their myths are the best informants about the people who worshipped them, and in looking through the Deity to understand the people, we learn even more about the Deity.

What we do know about the ancient Celts, based on their peers' writings, is that they were envied for their beautiful clothing and jewelry, but feared on the battlefield. They were criticized for indulging in booze and sensual pleasures, but also praised for their health and fitness. Some marveled at the Celtic society, where it was said no beggars could be found, and admired their extensive hospitality to friendly guests. Other accounts describe the Celts as shrewdly protective over their lands and tribes, wary of strangers, unabashedly willing to shed blood to defend what was theirs. Their religious world was equally passionate, and it was from this that Brigid's iron-strong legacy was born.

The ancient Celtic world was a massive civilization whose height of power occurred roughly 600 B.C.E. to 400 C.E. in Ireland and the British Isles, as well as what is now Portugal, northern Italy and Spain, France, southern Poland, and central Turkey. It was a melting-pot culture which originated from tribes that immigrated from extensive regions of the world, intermarrying with pre-Celtic indigenous peoples. Brigid likely began as a collection of Goddesses—some regional Stone Age Goddesses, some imported with immigrating tribes. In the way that streams feed rivers, these early Deities fed into Brigid—her own ancestral streams possibly tens of thousands of years old.

As Celtic culture grew, its pantheon exploded. One explorer counted over 400 Deities in the British Isles, alone. The names and myths of many were lost to time and eventually to religious conversion when Christianity moved in. The few that did find their way into written lore often did so centuries later through the pens of Roman explorers and Christian monks. Some were painted with a seemingly subjective slant as frightening characters that could have been the new religion's interpretation. Yet, some of the descriptions may have been somewhat accurate. Celtic Deities were literal representations of forces of nature which could be unpredictable and not always benevolent. Ocean Gods could supply food and travel, but could also flood coastal villages and swallow sailors. Sun Gods could nurture crops, but also hide behind a rain bank for months leaving the fields to rot. Celtic Goddesses were typically not gentle, loving mother-figures, but aggressive, voracious, highly sexual, even bloodthirsty. Ronald Hutton in *The Pagan Religions of the Ancient British Isles* points out that it is difficult to tell whether these were real reflections of the Goddesses, role models for Celtic women, fantasies of the Celtic men, or the nightmarish visions of the Roman explorers or the Christian monks who eventually wrote down the descriptions. In general, Celtic Gods and Goddesses were feared much more than beloved. A far cry from the sedate churches or ceremonial circles of later centuries, the religion of the ancient Celts was primal, wild, and fierce. Worship was less about reverence and more a line of defense against these Beings. Brigid's earliest worship may have originated out of fear.

Even as the Celtic culture grew, it remained far from homogenized. The numerous tribes retained their own regional practices, dialects, and customs, but there were still quite a few similarities. Most practiced *animism,* a belief that all things contain a cognizant spirit. Another commonality was a term for an exalted being: *Brig* or *Brid.* One medieval inventory listed ten different Brighids, twelve Brígs, and three known as both. This led researchers, Goddess lovers, and folklorists to believe that there once was a great Goddess named Brig (later, Brigid) and she ruled over all the Celtic world. In reality, Brig's literal meaning of "the Exalted One" or "The Great Lady" was frequently applied to female entities as well as women in positions of power. One example in Ireland was a first-century woman called Brigh who held office as a judge. It is less likely that the woman's name was Brigh and more likely that it referred to her position as a supreme judge who was also female. Brig and its variations were attributed to sacred items, places, and concepts, such as *Brig Ambue* (The Great Lady of Justice) or *Bríg Brigug* (The Great Lady Who Provides, a reference to fertile earth). The animist spirit was often female and so the title Brig was often applied to the spirits believed to inhabit sacred places such as wells and blacksmith shops. Practices of great renown such as the Bardic arts were also believed to contain feminine spirits, which influenced their cultivation. Over the centuries, foreign ears heard the term *Brig* and may have assumed it to be a singular Goddess who held jurisdiction over innumerable things. Over time, Brig popped up in various roles—large and small—in myth and lore, and eventually evolved into a singular, massively popular figure with highly diverse traits.

Brig, the Exalted One, was said to be so great that a human could only reach as high as her brass shoe. While Brig was spirit of many things, she was primarily the green earth itself. This should not be confused with being a Goddess "of" the earth. Brig was not a caretaker or steward. The earth was alive and cognizant. Brig was its spirit and the soil, rocks, hills, and rivers were her body. Today, images commonly associated with Brigid include three identical women, but these do not appear on any pottery, monuments, or artifacts from the pre-Roman Celtic era. For centuries, the Brig existed in word and worship of the landscape, alone. The Celts made few—if any—carved images of their Divine. If their Goddess could be seen in the earth they walked upon, was a carved image even necessary?

Eventually, Brig would emerge in chiseled stone. Statues of Brig appeared in what is now Britain, where she was called Brigantia. These carvings made their appearance as the Roman influence increased in the Celtic world. The Romans carved images of their Deities and likely inspired the process. Some of the first statues and etchings of the Celtic Deities were courtesy of the Romans, themselves. Brigantia's first images are quite similar to those of the Roman Goddess Minerva, a Patroness of wisdom, war, and urban living. Like Minerva images, Brigantia was depicted wearing a helmet and carrying a spear, but her trademark image was a jug of water, which Minerva was not seen carrying. The water image preserved her connection to the rivers and streams sacred to the Celtic world. Minerva was indelibly important to the Romans. Brigantia's strikingly similar depictions underscore her equal importance to the Celts. One theory suggests Brigantia was a sole invention of the Romans, looking for a local Goddess to identify with in their newly colonized land. Hearing "Brig . . . Brig . . ." on the tongues of the natives may have confused the Romans, leading them to assume there was a great regional Goddess named Brig rather than Brig being an animist-influenced title. Then again, maybe they were right.

THE EXALTED ONE IN IRELAND

Relations between the Romans and the Celts were tense. Both groups were pillagers and plunderers of one another's resources, and wars were frequent. After centuries of reciprocal "sackings," the Romans ultimately took control of much of the region by striking the spiritual and political nerve center of the Celtic world: the Druid caste. Some believe Brig, the Exalted One, was the patron Goddess of the Druids, which makes sense if one considers the exalted position the Druids had. The Druids were the priesthood and the ultimate authority of the Celtic world. Strabo (around 24 B.C.E.), described the Druids as three honored classes: Prophets, Philosophers, and Bards. Other writers of that era noted that, "No man speaks before a King, and no King speaks before a Druid." But as Roman rule gradually increased throughout most of Celtic world, the Druid priesthood was systemically disassembled and the Exalted One's presence diminished in the land named for Brigantia—Britain. Brig remained in folklore and customs throughout the region, but it was in Ireland where the Exalted One would ultimately thrive. It was there she was called *Brigid*.

Some believe that British Druids, fleeing Roman oppression, brought their Brig, as Brigantia, to Ireland where the Irish Druids quickly included her in their regional pantheon. Others argue that Brigid was in Ireland all along, her worship perhaps enhanced by the refugees who recognized their own versions of the Exalted One in her. Still others say Brigid was only ever the regional land Goddess of the Irish province of Leinster and never had anything to do with the Minerva-influenced Brigantia. The Romans never made it to Ireland, so while Brig in her many forms would dwindle in most areas, much about the Celtic world remained preserved in Ireland, including the Exalted One.

This figurine, from St. Bridget's Church at St. Brides Bay, Wales, is one of the few that depicts the Christian St. Brigid with the stang— a Druid's staff.

Celtic spirituality linked the number three with all things divine and so Brigid the Goddess began to appear in lore and image in triplicate form. Contemporary images of Brigid often depict her as maiden, mother, and crone, associating the three sisters with the phases of the moon: waxing, full, and waning, but this is not a correct correlation. Brigid has historically been considered a solar Deity and as three identical women of the same age, sometimes called the Three Brigid Sisters: Woman of Healing (*Ban leighis*), Woman of Smithwork (*Ban goibnechtae*), and Woman Poet (*Ban fhile*). In addition to being the living earth, Brigid was also seen as the living embodiment of spring. In Scottish folklore, Brigid was imprisoned in the Ben Nevis mountain by the Calleach, the Winter Hag, every year when winter set in and then released in the early days of spring. In other depictions, Brigid and the Calleach were the same Goddess with two faces—one comely and one haggard. Brigid was credited with milk production, which would occur around the beginning of February at the holiday of Imbolc, a word meaning "of milk." For this reason, she was also credited as a Patroness of sheep and cattle. Brigid's characteristics represented those held in highest regard by Celtic culture. Her prominent presence continued, even as Christianity crept into Ireland.

BRIGID: WARRIOR SAINT AND HISTORIC REBEL

As Christianity spread across Europe, the Gods of indigenous faiths were either disregarded by the Church or absorbed into folklore. Some were demoted to demons in the new Christian lore. Others were transformed into heroes of a legendary past where they continued to be revered with magick and significance. Still others, particularly those of paramount importance, were adopted as saints. The role of beloved saint was the next chapter for Brigid.

The idea of a beloved God or Goddess of ancient Pagan history turning into a saint can be a painful one for those who love old religions and Goddess worship. For many, the movement from God to saint may seem a demotion, although those who have loved and honored the saints would likely disagree. Particularly in the case of Brigid, the new saint lost few, if any, of her Goddess characteristics and was revered with power and prestige in Ireland on a level only rivaled by St. Patrick. St. Brigid was identified with the Christian Mother-Goddess figure of Mary, as "Mary of the Gaels," or sometimes "the Foster-Mother of Christ," and in some stories as Mary's midwife. With the exception of the archangels, very few saints enjoy such inclusion with the two most important figures in Catholic Christianity. Even so, St. Brigid is an unsaintly character, one known for screeching across battlefields or flagrant defiance against Church leaders.

St. Brigid is both historical figure and character of folklore and shared more than a name with her Pagan Goddess counterpart. It is through St. Brigid that the clearest glimpse into Brigid the Goddess can be found. The great cathedral of St. Brigid in Kildare, Ireland is believed to have been founded by the saint herself. It is widely accepted that the church was built upon an even older Pagan shrine, where a perpetual fire was kept in honor of the Goddess Brigid. Like the legacy of Brig, Brigid was probably a title rather than a name for a leading Druidess the Brig or Great Lady of Kildare. This Brigid oversaw the shrine's care, later leading its conversion from Pagan to Catholic. Perhaps the crafty leader saw a way to preserve veneration of the sacred sites under a seemingly inevitable Christian transformation and coordinated it on her own terms. The story goes that the Druidess-nun was consecrated as Bishop of Kildare by accident. According to legend, the Bishop Ibor, performing the liturgical rite, read from the wrong passage and gave Brigid a status of power unheard of for women, even in contemporary Catholicism. If the story is true, it was almost certainly not an accident. Druidesses commonly held high posts, although nuns did not. To keep the respected Druidess in a powerful position would have been to the Church's advantage, strengthening alliances with the local population. After her death, she became St. Brigid. Even in the new faith, Brigid remained exalted.

This character entered lore with the same ferocity and warriorship found in the Pagan Goddess, as well as relentless work against poverty. St. Brigid was known for giving anything she possibly could to those in need. After her death, this important lady was buried in the church of Kildare in an elaborate coffin and reportedly surrounded by treasures and gifts from the community. Shortly thereafter, grave robbers stripped the tomb of is riches. Although a sad crime when we consider what sorts of treasures history has lost, it is true to the legacy of the saint who, even in death, continued to give all that she had to those in need.

St. Brigid was sometimes said to have had a woman friend or fellow nun in the convent named Darlughdacha, the literal translation of which means "Daughter of the God Lugh," who herself became the leader of the Kildare abbey upon Brigid's death. Other stories say that Brigid was actually Darlughdacha and a daughter of the God Lugh, herself, Brigid being only her title. Brigid and Darlughdacha reportedly shared a bed each night. One day, Brigid caught Darlughdacha gazing at a passing warrior. Brigid demanded she walk in shoes packed with red-hot coals as penance—either in sanctity of her convent vows of chastity or possibly to subdue Brigid's personal jealousy, indicating that the two were lovers. The coals and the rage are among many, many other traits that resonate far more with a Pagan Fire and War Goddess than a standard saint. Additionally, the Church at Kildare has lost few of its Pagan roots. Kildare (*cill dara*) means "Church of the Oak Tree." Oak is not a tree regularly honored in Christian lore, nor are perpetual fires commonly dedicated to Catholic saints, yet both are prominent in the reverence of St. Brigid. The gap between the Pagan and Christian rites of Brigid are quite small indeed.

St. Brigid formed an important link in the religious and spiritual life of the first Irish Catholics in bridging their ancestral religion with the one newly imported. St. Brigid was known for her miracles of healing, care for animals—particularly livestock that produced milk, as did her Pagan incarnation—dedication to the poor, and fighting oppressive forces, including (and some-times especially) Church leaders. St. Brigid cannot be cast off as a modification of the Goddess. Rather, the canonization of Brigid as a Catholic saint preserved her and stands as a testimony of the Goddess's enduring importance.

BRIGID BEYOND IRELAND

Brigid's influence did not stop on the shores of her homeland. From the early 1700s to about the mid-1800s, nearly half a million Irish traded years of unpaid labor in exchange for passage to the Western Hemisphere, a process known as indentured servitude. Landowners, most often in Trinidad, French Guiana, and Suriname, would provide the indentured worker with clothing, food, and shelter. At the end of their agreed term of servitude, the worker could—in theory—walk away as a free person to pursue landownership and opportunity. Unfortunately, these promises were often empty and the workers faced frequent mistreatment and cruelty. Illness and death due to hunger, disease, and exposure was common.

Indentured servants worked and lived alongside enslaved Africans also brought over to work, but who did not have the prospect of eventual freedom. Practices and religious beliefs of the Irish and various African cultures were shared under these torturous conditions. The religion of Voudon (sometimes called Voodoo) was born in the Caribbean from the cohesion of these and indigenous island practices. Voudon is composed of spiritual beings called *Lwa* (also called Loa), which could be compared to exalted ancestors or a form of saints or angels. This is far from a comprehensive explanation of the world of Voudon, and I encourage those who are intrigued by this passage to seek out further knowledge. Approaching and sharing this material is tricky for me as a writer and Priestess. I have a deep love and respect for the practices, culture, and history of Voudon, yet am not an initiate of it, nor is it part of my ancestral heritage. Because of my lack of direct experience, I have not included Voudon practices or rituals in this book as I am without the founding to do them proper justice. Still, a good overview of the complex world of Brigid could not be complete without investigating Maman Brigitte.

Many Catholic saints whose devotees passed through the islands found new roles and life in the Voudon religion. Among them was St. Brigid who was reborn as the Lwa Maman Brigitte, the Lady of the Cemetery. Maman Brigitte is the only Lwa with white skin and red hair. She is sought for issues pertaining to justice or contacting the *Gede*—the ancestral spirits. Maman Brigitte is a tough character, often described as a profanity-spewing, hardened presence, yet still full of fierce love. She is made of a presence that could wrap someone up in the toughest, motherly embrace, or cut with a hidden blade if crossed. She is symbolized by a black rooster, and known for donning bright, clashing costumes, use of rancid profanity, and flagrant sexuality. Maman Brigitte lives in an oak tree in the cemetery and is married to Baron Samedi, a Lwa of the Dead. The first woman buried in any cemetery is called "The Brigitte" and considered sacred to Maman. Likewise, the first man buried in that cemetery is known as the Baron.

Maman is known to love a spicy rum drink called *piman,* which is infused with a combination of twenty-one hot peppers. This drink is often offered at circles honoring her as a way to test if a person is mounted by Maman Brigitte. The concoction is so intense that a mortal, living person could not hold the drink in their mouths without help from the Divine. Persons possessed by Maman are known to rub the hot rum on their genitals, another tell-tale sign of possession—if a mortal cannot hold the drink in their mouth, the drink is certainly not going to end up willingly on their privates without that Divine help. The practice referred to as being "mounted by" or "ridden by" a Lwa refers to a type of ritual possession akin to the way that a mortal person would ride a horse. The person is under complete control of the Lwa and is known to be able to perform certain feats unthinkable under normal circumstances. The festival of *Fet Gede* honors Maman Brigitte on November 1st, a date shared by the Celtic fire festival of *Samhain,* which was believed to be the day when the winter hag Cailleach whisked Brigid away until spring.

Some argue that Maman Brigitte's connections to Brigid are overblown or even contrived, citing that Brigid's fire and wells stand in too stark a contrast to Maman Brigitte's patronage of death and the cemetery. Others argue that the name, appearance, championship for justice, and connection to the oak are parallels too strong to ignore. There is a Voudon song that goes, "Maman Brigitte who came from England," which in considering Brigid's history as Brigantia may be even more basis for connection. On my last trip to the Kildare Cathedral, I asked the cemetery groundskeeper where I could find the grave of the first woman buried there. "St. Brigid herself was the first," he said. Brigid was her own Brigitte. Perhaps that connection made its way across the Atlantic and south to the Caribbean Islands, expanding the web of influence of both the revered Irish Fire Goddess and the beloved Lwa.

FOR MY PART . . .

Brigid was the first Goddess I met when I started my Pagan path. After attending a series of Brigid rituals and hearing personal stories about this Goddess's impact, I decided to give her a try. I was at the end of my college career, and because she was a Goddess of the arts and my major was theater, it seemed a good match. During these early days of praying to Brigid and lighting red candles for her in my tiny college apartment, I took an elective creative writing class and discovered that writing, more than theater, was my real passion. Yet despite my love for writing short stories, I was thoroughly stuck on how to do it. I felt the story in me, but the words would not come. It was like turning the key in a dead ignition. I knew the story was in there, somewhere. Getting it to work was the problem. Frustrated, I performed a creativity spell to help move the process along. As part of my spell, I offered to write a book dedicated to Brigid, if she would help me to give the story life.

In the days that followed, the hopelessly constipated short story pulled itself together. I would wake with dialogue and action played out before me like a teleprompter. When I turned it in, not only did my professor and classmates love it, the story was published by a national magazine and nominated for an important fiction award. Problematically for me, I forgot about the book I promised to Brigid. Perhaps it's not surprising that I had little luck with fiction again after that initial success. I was frustrated and blocked once again.

I moved to New York to look for the lost inspiration in the underground performing and writing scene. I found inspiration of a different kind in the members of the first coven I would lead, which would eventually grow into one of the largest Pagan communities in the northeast of the United States, but I still could not write. Our first circle took place at Brigid's holiday of Imbolc and has since attracted droves of lovers of Brigid and Brigid devotees. My work with Brigid took me to Ireland several times and New Orleans once. With each class, circle, ritual, or eerily synchronistic meeting with a new friend in Brigid, I fell deeper in love with her mystery and magick. Still, creativity on the page remained stunted. Finally, in a way greater than studies or sacred site visits, Brigid's true nature came to me through the form of the anvil when I became her Priestess.

Toward the end of my twenties, I was in a situation common to many persons, and unfortunately, many young women. My purpose, magick, and faith were funneled into a hopeless romantic relationship. Like a toddler screaming for cotton candy, I fixated on it as though it were the only thing in the entire universe, ignoring any signs or warnings that it, like cotton candy, was fragile, empty, and composed more of whimsy than the kind of nurturing and sustaining love needed for a true partnership. It shaped all of my plans for the future, absorbed all spare time as well as quite a bit of money. Every spell focused on keeping us together. Every prayer, thought, and combination of the two was directed toward keeping that relationship going. Immersed in a city drenched with art, culture, and friendships, I shut out these influences to focus personal, magickal, and spiritual energy into the relationship. I felt Brigid's presence turn from a warm and boisterous guide to an eerie, prickly one, like the sense one gets in a room full of quietly angry people. In my heart, I knew that Brigid's energies did not align with the situation. Even deeper down, I knew it was wrong, too. My prayers turned to explanations, as if to prove that I was "more right" about this than the Goddess. Eventually, Brigid's presence went silent. I thought this meant I finally had her on my side, but the silence was more like foreboding, as in the proverbial calm before the storm. This was the energy in the days surrounding my initiation to Brigid. Still, I traveled to Ireland to formally dedicate to her.

The ceremony was simple, but the aftermath was not. Prior to the ritual, I was left alone in a room to meditate. In the quiet and darkness, I heard Brigid's voice coming up from inside me, firing verbal bullets about my current path and future, not the deep, loving wisdom I'd come to know in my meditations. I blamed insecurities. It couldn't be Brigid. Brigid was on my side, wasn't she? I was surely just a little nervous. But when I was taken out of the meditation and into the circle, the presiding Priestess whacked me across the face and eerily continued the same verbal barrage I heard in my private mediation only moments before, only the words were clearer: "WHAT ARE YOU DOING? STOP WHAT YOU ARE DOING! STOP! STOP!" At the end of the barrage, the Priestess placed a gentle hand on my cheek and she said, "This will never happen to you, again."

I spent the following day sobbing into my friends' living room carpet. The morning after the initiation, thanks to the oracle that is social media, I discovered that back in the States, my relationship was over and with it, all the plans I'd so diligently made. Worse, the break-up ended a nearly lifelong friendship, which proved the most painful sacrifice of all. In retrospect, it was the greatest day of my life, but at that point it felt like the end. To soothe my shattered nerves, my friends took me for a walk in the forest. Up above, a storm cloud took the undeniable shape of an anvil. Brigid had a hand in that nasty business, I was sure of it. In the following months, I let go and "let Brigid." While my past had a six-mile roll-call of break-ups, this one was different. Instead of dissolving into my old, angry coping manner of "you-go-girl" pep-talk to myself about "other fishies in that big ol' sea" that would unravel into wine, and tears, and chasing after yet another assured heartbreak, I sat with Brigid. I examined my choices. I reflected on the lies I'd absorbed and told. I owned the harm I caused myself and others and then looked at a decade's worth of habits that set up all those glass walls in a prime place for one trusted sledgehammer to crash—why I surrounded myself with people who hurt me or themselves, why I wandered through jobs without pursuing something fulfilling, why I wrote about the sensational instead of the words and experiences my heart screamed for. One by one, I allowed Brigid to pound away the hurtful things blocking my path. Each pound left me stronger and healed.

Within a few months, I was accepted into a graduate school program. My coven emerged from a tiny fringe group casually meeting in members' apartments to the prominent presence that it is now. Best of all, I met the man with whom I am now partnered who himself is a devotee of Brigid—the relationship fulfilling in ways the previous one, or any before that, had never been. Despite my initial anger and pain, epitomized by the anvil I saw in the sky, I had no doubt that the losses were directly connected to Brigid and that it would eventually be for the best. Indeed, it was. I now call this period "my time on the anvil." I could probably dedicate a whole book to my anvil time, and maybe someday I will. But this book isn't about me. It's about Brigid and hopefully you, too.

Eventually, it was time to fulfill my own promise to Brigid.

Over the years, I received one same message from Seers, Priestesses, and in readings: "Where is the book? Where is the book?" I assumed this book was one already written, locked away in the rumored secret libraries of the Vatican, and it was up to me to break in, find the book, and release The Truth to the public. My graduate school was at a funky locked-crossroads due to the logistical infeasibility that comes with needing to work to pay for school, but being unable to go to school because of work. One night, a fellow Priestess of Brigid who knew nothing of the promises I'd made to Brigid (because at that point, *I'd* forgotten the promises I made to Brigid) looked at me with fiery eyes that weren't hers and said, "Why do you think I've frozen your life? Why do you think you can't finish anything? You promised me a book and I won't help you with anything until you get it to me." The Priestess then closed her eyes, shook her head, and returned to our previous conversation as if the whole thing had never happened. My mind burned with the flash-fire memory of lighting a red candle in college and promising Brigid a book if she would help me with that one short story. A few weeks later, I started writing the book you are now reading.

Let this serve as a testament to anyone who might want to work with Brigid: do not make your promises lightly as Brigid will surely not take them lightly!

Brigid's energy is real. Brigid's magick works. I have seen people make offerings to her, whether at wells in Ireland or in the center of an urban Imbolc rite, and borne witness to their manifestation. Every spell I have worked through Brigid has come to manifestation. Everything I have asked has ultimately been fulfilled—not always in the manner I initially wanted, but fulfilled nonetheless. When I have been in need and not sure where the need's fulfillment would come from, it has been consistently met through perfect synchronicity.

This book is an attempt to share with other Brigid lovers an opportunity to relish her beautiful myths, explore her vast history, and learn new ways to connect with her. I also ask you, the reader, to keep in mind that much of this book also reflects Irish history, culture, and lore, but you are reading it from a foreigner's perspective. Like most Americans, I have a healthy dose of Irish in my DNA mix, but the branches of my family tree stemming from Ireland have been on American soil for over a hundred years. My upbringing, experiences, culture, and family practices vary every bit as widely from those of my Irish friends as they do from my Jamaican, Haitian, British, Italian, Argentine, or Mexican friends. To pretend to be otherwise or to pretend to know what it means to have been born on and experienced the tides of the land, culture, and historic events of a region undermines the experiences of those who have. I am not an academic. I am not a historian. I am not an anthropologist or an archeologist. I am a Priestess, a writer, and a glutton for history, folklore, and mythology. Above all, I am a lover of Brigid. I write this book with humility and respect for the cultures and regions my beloved Goddess comes from. I have tried to present the stories and theories with as much objectivity as possible. I have made very clear the few places where I have taken creative license for the purpose of providing tools for better understanding Brigid's role in the myths.

If you are indeed reading this, it means I have finally fulfilled my promise and can only hope that it not only serves it well, but provides tools for anyone who seeks the history, mystery, and magick found in the Lady of the Wells, the Flame, and the Earth itself: the great Goddess Brigid. Throughout the book, I use Brigid and St. Brigid interchangeably as I do not believe them to be separate characters, but rather evolutions of the same. In reading through the myths and stories, allow yourself to be led with the heart rather than the head. Notice what pieces of story touch or excite you. Also notice what pieces make you wish to resist. Often, the sense of resistance points to where the work really needs to happen. Above all, enjoy it.

Blessed be your journey. I am honored to be a part of it.

The anvil cloud. Does it look like an anvil to you?

CHAPTER 2

The Origins of Brigid

Lady of the Well, the Forge, and the Green Earth,
I seek you.
Warm my heart with your perpetual flame,
Heal my wounds with your gentle waters,
Cradle me in your mantle when I can walk no more,
Brigid, I seek you.

—Brigid, I Seek You

Brigid's origin myths bring no peace to the logical mind. She appears as an important daughter of a God in one myth, but the wife of that God in a different telling, while vanishing completely in a third version. Which version is the right version? Does any myth from any source even have a "right" telling? The various versions tell us about the storyteller. Brigid's myths had many tellers and, therefore, many versions. Stories varied widely, circulated through oral tradition in local vernacular. As Christian monks later recorded the myths, characters were often augmented to fit Christian ideals. Still, these subjective details are but a thin veneer on the Pagan origins and the different tellings do not negate each other. If we allow them, the varied stories can weave a complex and beautiful tapestry of history and culture. Discovering myth can be a deeply personal experience. Through myth, we can come to new understandings about our own journeys. In the following stories, I have included my thoughts about their potential truths and Brigid's role, but my thoughts are not meant to be the final authority. If they enhance your experience, wonderful! But if they do not, ignore them. You will ultimately be your own authority on the myths' meanings and messages.

Image of St. Ffraid (St. Brigid) at St. Ffraid's Church in Trearddur Bay. One legend of St. Brigid says that she arrived in Wales on a piece of turf, landing at Trearddur Bay. The green patch at her feet is that piece of turf, a striking image of a Mother Goddess. She holds a perpetual flame in her hand.

BRIGID: MOTHER OF CREATION

At the beginning of time, when the world was dark and quiet, a great tree grew from the new soil. It was the tallest and the strongest tree that ever was, called Bile: The Sacred Oak. The sacred waters from above nurtured and cherished this great tree. The waters were called Dana. Through the conjugation of Dana and Bile, there dropped two giant acorns. From the first acorn sprang the Dagda, "The Good God." From the second emerged Brigantu, or Brigid, "The Exalted One." The Dagda and Brigid gazed upon their new world in awe. They chose to create order in the world, and to populate the beautiful place with the children of Dana, the divine Mother Goddess who had nourished them from the beginning.

Brigid and the Dagda took to a fertile valley, one that faced outward to the eastern sea, where the waters of the divine Mother Dana would nourish the land on which they lived. They named these waters Danavius, known forever after as the mighty Danube. Brigid and the Dagda built the four greatest cities the world had ever seen: Falias, Gorias, Finias, and Murias. In these cities, the children of Dana would thrive for all time. These children named the Dagda as their father and the "Father of All Gods." Brigid was the wise Mother, having taken the great knowledge of the world from the Sacred Oak called Bile.

Brigid was hailed for teaching the children of Dana healing, craftsmanship, and poetry, but most of all, she showed her children that true wisdom was first garnered from the feet of Dana, the Mother Goddess, and only where the water meets the land.

—Inspired by "The Ever Living Ones," in *The Mammoth Book of Celtic Myths and Legends* by Peter Berresford Ellis

Much of Celtic mythology stems from stories of mythical invaders and colonizers of Ireland, called *Tuatha de Danann*, meaning "The Folk of the God whose Mother is Dana." Dana is one of the Great Irish Mother Goddesses, but in many cases she and Brigid are interchangeable. In other myths, the Gods came to Ireland through ships in the air, from four great otherworldly cities. The passengers included the Dagda and Brigid. The Dagda (sometimes called Eochaidh, known as "The Good God" or

"Divine Father"), who provided food and prosperity to people, has a recurring role in Celtic mythology as a herald of life. He had a cauldron so full of nourishing food that no one would ever walk away from it unsatisfied. As a Father-King of humankind, he presided over a golden age in which dew fell instead of rain and each year was fruitful.

The Dagda was an exception to the Celts' view of their Gods as embodiments of dangerous forces. He represented life's potential for plenty. The Dagda and the Tuatha de Danann represented civilization while their enemies, the Fomorians, represented perilous aspects of the wild environment: foul weather, famine, and dangerous animals. As King of the Tuatha, the Dagda led the fight against the forces embodied in the Fomorians who endangered the lives of the people.

Brigid is often the daughter of the Dagda, but here, Brigid stands as a partner in the creation of civilization. In this myth, Brigid shapes the potential provided by Bile and Dana into usable and accessible commodities for the people. She gives them the tools of civilization to live a strong quality of life, but also teaches utmost respect for the original source of life. She lives in harmony, not competition, with the Dagda, setting a precedent for how all children of Dana can live together. Water, in Celtic lore, was a source of ancestral wisdom. With this in mind, Brigid stands on the border of the lessons of the past and the mysteries of the future, symbolized by finding true wisdom at the water's edge, where these two realms meet. Meditating on this myth of Brigid, the Mother of Creation, can help a seeker envision the potential possible for any aspect of his or her life.

Reflection: Brigid had nothing when she began her journey in this world, just hope and awareness. Yet she saw the potential in the nothing. Without the tools to provide, she made the tools to provide. Imagine for a moment that all things surrounding us could

potentially be used in our favor. Brigid could have seen the water
as a flooding, damaging element and the great tree as an obstacle.
Instead, she saw opportunity. How might we see our obstacles as
opportunity? Imagine for a moment that everything that hinders is
actually helping. What feats could we then accomplish?

DAUGHTER OF THE RIVER

A magick well once existed in a place beneath nine magick hazel
trees. These trees held all the wisdom in the world. No one, not
even the Highest Gods, was permitted to approach the well, except
for the Salmon of Knowledge. The fish swam in its waters and ate
the nuts the trees dropped into them, which gave the fish all the
wisdom in the world. One day, the Goddess Boann was seized by
fervent curiosity. She approached the well as she could not stay
away, and walked around it counter-clockwise. The well's waters
rose at her and drove her away in a rushing flood. Boann was
swept along, and in the flood, lost an arm, eye, and leg. The waters
never returned to the well, and Boann's body became the river
called Boyne. The Dagda visited Boann in her riverbed, and by
standing with one foot on both shores, had several children with
her: Angus Mac Og, who gave love to the world; Mider, who ruled
the dead; Ogma, who taught the world literature and writing;
Boadb the Red, who would one day succeed his father as King of
the Gods; and Brigid, who brought poetry and the forge. To this
day, the Boyne is populated by the wandering salmon, looking for
the hazelnuts of wisdom they lost so long ago.

—Inspired by traditional tale

Boann (also called Bóinn) is what some might call a *Genius
Loci*, a living spirit of a physical place. To the ancient Celts, all
natural places, especially areas of water, contained embodied

spirits. Boann would have been the name for the spirit of the Boyne. The river was undeniably important to the Celtic community, for practicality's sake as well as spiritual means. From these flowing waters came the source of the tools necessary for the people of the region to not only live, but thrive. The salmon run provided bountiful food, and the river's waters provided transportation and sanitation. Smiths would have needed the water to temper the forged iron. It makes sense that the Boyne, the source of life for the region, also served as the birth of Brigid. The Dagda returns in this myth, likely representing the sun and the rain, whereas Boann as the riverbed represents water, but also the earth. The sun, rain, river, and land in combination produced the conditions necessary for the community's survival.

Brigid and her siblings represent things that make human lives worth living: love through Angus Mac Og, literature and communication through Ogma, legacy through Mider of the Dead, and self-sovereignty through Boadb the Red. Brigid contributes not only tools of society (represented by the forge), but also gifts of spiritual life. Ogma may have contributed literature, but poetry was considered a spiritual material of its own right that not only told stories, but preserved history and culture. The gift of the forge represented the technology crucial to survival, and was also considered magickal. The transformation of useless pieces into something of great value under the smith's hammer was considered an act of the Gods. Brigid's contributions of commerce and spirit were gifts both practical and divine.

A river may sound like a gentle mother, invoking images of a lazy water trail winding through lush countryside. Yet the Boyne river has a treacherous undercurrent and dangerous whirlpools. One regional legend says the Boyne takes seven lives a year. Boann took monumental risk by defying the Gods to satisfy her thirst for knowledge. She gave all of herself to her challenge and, through that, found a new identity and left an immense legacy.

Reflection: Ultimately, this is a story about sacrifice. No great reward is without great risk, as the myth of the treacherous river reminds us. In this myth, Brigid embodies the gifts that emerge after upheaval. Whether self-created or circumstantial, after the current has passed, we are stronger and better equipped to navigate the tides and whirlpools of our own existence. What have you being willing to sacrifice for great reward? What would you? What would you not?

DAUGHTER OF THE WARRIOR QUEEN

The Dagda dwelt in Glen Etin in the north, and met a woman on the day which was a year before he was to fight a great battle. She was washing, standing with one of her feet to the south of a great river, and the other, to the river's north. She wore nine loosened tresses on her head. The Dagda spoke with the woman, who was the Morrighan, Goddess of War. They took to bed. The place of their bedding was called the Bed of the Couple ever afterward, and the result of their time in the bed was Brigid. They lay together all night and come the morning, the Morrighan revealed a prophecy to the Dagda. His enemy, the Fomorians, would land at the Ford of Unius. She vowed to destroy the King of the Fomorians, by draining his life blood and valor away, ensuring the Dagda's victory.

—INSPIRED BY TRADITIONAL TALE AS WRITTEN IN
Brigid: Goddess, Druidess, and Saint by Brian Wright

This is one of the older Brigid myths, although she does not always appear in it. In this version, her mother is the Morrighan, the Goddess of war and death. The Morrighan was said to embody all that terrifies, particularly war and death. She was represented by a crow or raven, the birds commonly seen on the battlefield to feed on the remains of the dead. Despite these frightening images, the Morrighan was not typically feared as a Demon-Goddess. In the time of the Celts, war was common and lives were short. War wounds, infection, and disease frequently meant a slow, excruciating death. Morbid as it may seem, the sight of the ravens might have been welcome as it meant the end of suffering was nigh. The Morrighan represented an unavoidable yet respected facet of ancient Celtic life and her presence could also mean peace after turmoil and trauma. In many myths, she prophesies the outcome of battles and warns of future catastrophes, making her an important ally even in her most terrifying guises.

The Death Goddess and God of Life may seem an unlikely pair, yet they certainly function together well. Meeting the Warrior Queen in the river could have been an ominous sign for the Dagda. Seeing a woman washing at the river is a bad omen for a warrior preparing to go off to battle, suggesting that the woman is washing the bloodied clothes from soon-to-be fallen warriors. The Dagda could have fled from the sight, thinking it meant his own death was imminent. Perhaps he had more courage, being a God, or maybe he is an example of taking charge of the circumstances, no matter how frightening they may be. Not only is he undeterred, he has the courage to court her affections. Unlike tales from different pantheons (think of Greek Gods chasing and "ravaging" Goddesses or mortal women), the Dagda does not force himself on the Morrighan but charms her. Although their pillow talk is not particularly romantic, the two become the ultimate power couple. The Morrighan's wisdom is invaluable to the Dagda's battle plan and in the ancient Celtic world, Druidesses were often sought for their prophecies in the outcomes of battle. The Morrighan embodies this important community role. We don't know whether she is aware that she is pregnant with Brigid when she heads off to battle, or even if that would concern her, but away she goes to ensure her lover's success. A love of mutual respect and support binds the two characters and from it, Brigid is born.

Reflection: Brigid has her own canon of warrior myths, yet in this case, her own conception came about during a moment of peace. More so, Brigid came to be through an incident of facing fears and embracing the natural tides of life—not avoiding them. While in the other myths, Brigid provides tools needed for a higher quality of life, her role in this myth is to remind us that there is no gain or improvement without journeying through a place of fear, and sometimes even destruction. The third player in the triage of death and life is rebirth. If her mother is the herald of death and her father that of life, Brigid becomes the rebirth that occurs after all other things have been torn away.

In truth, we all come from unlikely scenarios. Out of thousands of human egg cells and millions of sperm cells, each of us came from the unlikely pairing of two cells who found each other solely by chance, most of whose kin will never find union or regenerate. We survived birth, infancy, and however many years between birth and the time you read these words. Layer in whether you suffered illness or accident, or otherwise. What extraneous circumstances occurred that meant your life was to be? Thinking in the present . . . what forces or elements scare you that, if you dared, you could unify with to make something great?

MEDITATION: THE MYTHS AND US

The following meditation is designed for you to explore how your own journey might connect to Brigid's myths and characters. If possible, this exercise is best done in a fetal position.

Breathe. Look for tensions in your body. Where you find the tension, breathe into it and allow your limbs to go soft. Allow your thoughts to fade away. If mental chatter surfaces, simply allow it to move along without following it or forcing it out. If your environment is noisy, acknowledge the sounds without blocking or following them.

Draw your attention to your heart. Breathe deeply and evenly and, as you do, pay attention to its rhythm. Be aware of things your heart may be experiencing at the moment—physically or emotionally, without judgment, analysis, or justification. Simply bear witness to your heart's present experience.

Allow yourself to see a gate in the area where your heart resides. Notice its shape and colors. Is it locked? Is it open? Unlatch the gate. If it is locked, breathe into the moment until the gate allows you to open it.

What do you see on the other side of your heart gate? Without judging or analyzing, take note of the images of the environment that you see. When you are ready, step through the gate.

In this new environment, you become aware of the presence of trickling water. Follow the sound. Slowly, it increases in volume and eventually, the source of this running water appears before you. Notice its colors, its depth, and breadth. If you feel it is safe to do so, touch the waters with a toe or foot. Now is not the time to fully submerge into the water, but to merely spend time with it. Take note of feelings, memories, senses, and even messages that may come about while you sit with this water.

Beneath the surface of the water, you notice movement. Watch as it begins to shape into delicate, swimming figures. These are the wandering Salmon of Knowledge. Sit with them for a while. What are they doing? Be present with the image.

You become aware of a presence beside you. It is a woman, strong and fit, with powerful hands and shoulders, and hair braided into nine tresses. She wears a golden necklace, bright as the sun, twisted into intricate fashion. Her tunic contains many colors. Notice them. She is washing something in the water. Be in communion with her presence. Approach her, softly and gently, and see what it is she is washing in the water. Speak to her, if you feel desire to do so, with respect and deference. She may choose to speak to you. If she does, listen. If she does not, simply be present with her image.

Far off in the distance, you hear the popping and crackling of a fire. In the air, a faint smell of a delicious meal entices you. Thanking the woman for the time spent, you walk away from her and from the water. Between you and the sound of fire is a thick forest. You can smell food. Between the trees, you see an orange glow and the occasional spark whirling upward. As you weave your way through the trees, the fire becomes clearer, warmer. The scent of food is stronger and more enticing. You may sense or see the presence of animals or other creatures in the woods. Take note of them, but continue to make your way to the fire and the meal.

When you reach the fire, you notice a man sitting beside it. He is both aged and timeless, wrapped in fur and crowned with gold. Over the fire sits a giant pot with something delicious inside, simmering furiously. Notice the furs the man is wearing. Be present with him for a moment. If you feel the need, speak to him with deference and respect. He may speak to you. If he does not, simply be present with his image for a time.

Behind the man and the fire, a worn path leads through the forest. Thanking the man for his time, walk away from the fire and deeper into the thickening trees. The air grows chilly as you walk along, farther away from the fire. Again, take note of animals or other presences you see in the forest. The soil darkens. The forest grows quiet, wilder, thicker. As you walk, the branches and limbs close in on you. You must fight and wrestle your way through the brush.

After a time, the woods thin out and the path widens. The forest comes to a clearing and, in the midst of it, is a single great tree so tall its top disappears into the clouds. The trunk is thick and knotted—it would take dozens of linked hands to encircle it. Its roots are fed by a dark, reflective pool of water, silent and still as the dawn but black as night. It stands at the place where the water meets the land. Brigid herself appears in a green cloak with the shining rays of the sun streaming from her head. She beckons you to the water's edge. Be present with her image. Approach the water's edge with an open heart and mind. Listen for the words of the waters of Dana and the wisdom of Brigid. If you do not hear anything, simply be present in this place.

When you have received and explored all that you wish, thank Brigid and offer thanks for the experience. Breathe deeply and become aware of the space of your heart. Allow the images to fade from view. Pull your awareness back into your heart and surrounding body. Become aware of your physical surroundings and sensations.

When you are ready, open your eyes and be present with your own environment.

This meditation is designed to be open-ended and fluid. Images and colors may shift and that is perfectly valid. Some may see abstract images of family, which can either be warming or upsetting, depending on personal history. Some may see little or nothing at all the first time they do this. If few or no images come to light, try again at another time. Taking note of certain images is important. What the woman is washing may indicate something in need of healing or completion. Animals seen in the woods may be Spirit or Soul Animals. Animal imagery is subjective to the individual. Seeing a fox for one person may mean something very different to another. Likewise, the fur the man is wearing may represent a need to embody the qualities of a certain kind of animal. Allow yourself to respond naturally to the images, if they are present. For further information on Brigid's Spirit Animals, please refer to Chapter 9. The meal in the cauldron is meant to symbolize what is good and nourishing for your soul. If these images were clear to you, it might be a good practice to incorporate their symbolic meanings into your daily life. Some images may be cryptic, but should be noted, anyway. Likely, they will come to make sense at another time.

Meditations are subjective. Some do not work for everyone. If your first attempt did not reveal much in the way of imagery or information, try again later. These are not tasks to be checked off and there is no prize or achievement implied in these works. The point of them is to explore and uncover.

Above all, remember to enjoy the journey.

CHAPTER 3

Brigid the Healer:
Lady of Sacred Waters

I will lead you home,
I will guide you back,
My waters will carry thee,
My flame will guide thee.

—"SEA SONG FROM BRÍD," Gemma McGowan

For the last several years, I've assisted in leading tours of the sacred sites of Ireland. Newgrange, Tara, the Kildare Cathedral and its fire shrine ... these are the places that excite potential tour members, naturally. They are main attractions, but repeatedly it is the holy wells—places of power, magick, and healing—that transform souls. Tears are shed as clouties are tied to the matronly thorn trees. Raw-hearted prayers are uttered and water is collected in bottles that held lunchtime bubbly refreshment as a souvenior of a magickal time. When we journey back to our various homes at the end of the tour, the main attraction sites are relished with great joy, but the wells and their power are almost inexplicable, recounted not through words, but with damp eyes and glowing faces. The wells are the embodiment of Brigid the Healer, a natural gift of the earth for peace and renewal.

A Brigid well in County Meath, Ireland.

Water has long been an integral part of Brigid worship and practice. The ancient Celts considered natural water sources sacred, mystical, and full of secrets. Their myths frequently included trickster Gods and Goddesses luring humans to watery depths, wild horses bounding from wave crests, and immense cities at the bottom of the seas. Lakes, rivers, bogs, and the sea were so revered that tremendous offerings of ornate swords, jewelry, or other riches were thrown into their depths as a method of honoring—or appeasing—spirits of the watery area. Some believe that the custom of throwing coins into wishing wells originated from this practice. Water certainly earned its reverence. Open water, the ocean in particular, contained inherent danger. For this reason, water was considered a portal to the Otherworld. Later Grail legends may have stemmed from these early beliefs.

Celtic pantheons included numerous individual water Deities, so while not all lakes, streams, and seas were immediately attributed to the Exalted One, Brigid would forever hold a firm connection to watery places. Variations of *Brig* were lent to a number of rivers in the Celtic world; Braint in Anglesey for one example, Brent in England for another.

Braint River in Anglesey, Wales.

Even after her British image was merged with Minerva, Brigantia's earliest depictions showed her pouring water from a jug. This may be a connection to the "safer face" of water—water that can be used for human consumption. This denotes Brigid's oldest and most primary connection to water: that of the natural well.

Wells held a miraculous role in the old world. A clean water source springing naturally from the ground was seen as a gift from the Divine. Clean water was not only a source for drinking, it was a beacon of sanitation and therefore, health. Because of their natural ability to heal, wells carved a place into consciousness and lore as magickal. After Europe's conversion to Christianity, many magick wells became holy wells but lost none of their mystical identity. Churches were constructed near wells for the access to water, but also for their draw as places of power and pilgrimage. These wells continue to be sought for their special properties, particularly for healing. Some are tucked in manicured churchyards; others sit hidden at the end of quiet roads, barely noticeable. Some wells even require treacherous climbs up rock hillsides and cliffs. While most contemporary wells are linked to Catholic saints, a little research will often link the well to a pre-Christian Deity. Throughout Ireland and other parts of the British Isles, thousands of healing wells are dedicated to Brigid.

Most wells contain a "pattern"—a ritual unique to a sacred site, performed to tap into the location's power. These patterns are believed to be direct links to the site's Pagan past. In the case of wells, this may include walking around the well in a certain direction, reciting a prayer, or making a libation in a certain form such as throwing a coin over a shoulder. Well visitors may anoint themselves or others with the healing waters. They may also tie trinkets representing the need for healing, such as a photo of an ill person, to the shrine or tree. Some wells are known for specific ailments, such as St. Kiernan's well in County Meath, which is sought for curing foot problems. Visitors often soak their feet in the water or leave socks at the shrine for podiatric health. Brigid's wells tend to be all-purpose, sought for a plethora of types of healing. Because of Brigid's patronage of motherhood, many approach her wells to pray for children.

Brigid's well in Kildare, Ireland. Photo courtesy of Elizabeth Guerra-Walker.

Water's spiritual power is not lost outside of the Celtic corner of the world. The idea of water—river torrents, natural hot springs, the ocean's waves, even the warm water of a soothing bath—heals ragged nerves and soothes souls. In fact, I am writing this on the morning of my community's Summer Solstice Rite, which we have entitled, "The Cauldron of Empowerment." We are expecting a great crowd to make a pilgrimage to an off-beat area of Brooklyn to find communion with the Divine reflected through the medium of water and the Cauldron. Clean water is a gift. In many parts of the world, clean water is not easily available or available at all. Despite technological developments, clean water is still a fundamental part of human existence. Without clean water, we have no health or future.

Brigid's continued presence in contemporary spirituality is a testament to the deeply rooted human belief in the power of water to heal, restore, and support life. Even those who do not live in proximity to her sacred wells can work with Brigid's well spirit. If geography is not your friend, mythology and imagination will be. To know Brigid's Healing Well, one must first be open to one's own healing, which calls for a pilgrimage of its own.

A Brigid well outside Mullingar, Ireland.

THE WELL OF HEALING

Two lepers came to visit Brigid at her sacred well in Kildare and asked for healing. She agreed, instructing them to bathe one another in the well until their skin healed. However, after one was healed, he refused to bathe the other as the sight of his former ailment disgusted him. He refused to touch his friend to bestow the healing he had just received. Witnessing the unkind act, Brigid was so angry that her fury caused his ailment to return. She wrapped her green mantle around the other and healed him completely.

—INSPIRED BY TRADITIONAL TALE

Reflection: It's tempting to believe a misfortune is a freak occurrence and once we move past it, we are forever rid of it. We are anxious to flee what might resemble previous pain. But if we flee, did we learn? Are we in danger of repeating mistakes that put our health in the poor position in the first place? Are we ignoring advice on improving a chronic condition? How can we revisit our pain with courage, as a reminder of how to stay on the path of healing?

Healing is a journey and not an easy one. Particularly in matters of physical ailments, the journey to health can be frustrating and exhausting, especially if the condition is chronic. Still, no healing will find its way to the ailing person unless the healing is sought. The person must seek healing just as the lepers sought Brigid. Like symbolic lepers, we make our own pilgrimages to a healing source—be that source a physician, a therapist, or a healing well. Sadly, not all ailments can be healed. Some chronic illnesses can be managed, but not cured. Some ailments are deadly, but fatal illness is a natural part of living existence and, in truth, how most of our lives will eventually end. Yet, if we don't at least try to overcome our illnesses, we are not being true to our evolutionary human nature as relentless problem-solvers.

Emotional and spiritual injuries must be taken with as much seriousness as those of the physical sense. If they are untreated, they themselves can end up as physical sickness. All healing takes time, but at a certain point (particularly in emotional matters), we must choose to heal our wounds. Seeking healing involves a sense of surrender, admission of our limitations, and accepting wholeness. Be it emotional, physical, or spiritual, the healing journey cannot be taken alone. The point when usual treatment options are exhausted is often the space when a person, as the saying goes, "Lets go and lets God." Those who choose to "Let go and let Brigid" frequently find their healing complete, via a radically transformative sense. Some say they cannot recognize their new lives afterward. Again, also as the saying goes, results may vary.

The exercises that follow are not meant to cure physical ailments on their own. However, they may inspire new avenues of treatment or at the very least, alleviate anxiety about the ailment.

MAKING THE JOURNEY TO THE WELL

The decision to visit the healing well, whether actual or symbolic, is itself an enormous step toward healing. As mentioned above, the pilgrimage to physical wells can be grueling. What may be even harder is accepting the need to seek the well in the first place. Pilgrimages usually begin when something within a person is lost, harmed, or disjointed. It can be difficult to accept that an injury has taken place. We do not like to think that we may be weakened by an experience, or that our condition is such that we need help to overcome it. Sometimes, we have suffered for so long that pain becomes a way of life and we forget that a better life is possible. Seeking spiritual help for healing is often a last resort.

If you live far from a healing well, you can still make pilgrimage to bodies of water in your region. Your region's water may or may not be known for healing qualities, but the journey will be the same. Your well could be a river, an ocean, or even an artificial pond. I make pilgrimages to the Hudson River down the street from my apartment when the need arises. The best sources are natural ones, but any source of water given reverence and sacredness will respond in kind.

On your pilgrimage, treat every step of your journey as part of the work. Small things normally unimportant may suddenly have great significance (e.g., the sight of an animal, the snippet of a passing conversation, a particular song on the car radio or iPod). Approach your journey to the well with open eyes and ears. *Take precautions for your safety.* While some pilgrimages will involve risk, don't create danger. Let someone know where you are going, be aware of your surroundings, and perform your pilgrimage by daylight. If you feel you absolutely must go to a secluded area or at nighttime, bring along a trusted friend who understands the nature of the pilgrimage, and can be there to assist in case you need help.

If you cannot travel to a water source, you can create your own well at home. I do this if the weather is bad or if I want to practice late at night. Fill a bowl with water and add a few generous pinches of sea salt. Include healing herbs or oils. Lavender is a common herb for healing, as are eucalyptus and sage. I enjoy using essential oil of black pepper, wintergreen or birch oil, and arnica. Research into the nature of healing herbs and oils will help you. What is the herb or oil known for? Does it mirror the qualities your work needs? Most importantly, is it poisonous or are you allergic to it? While some poisonous herbs or plants have medicinal benefits, do not use them without proper supervision or training. Consider including slices of apple. Apples are sacred to Brigid and are a good, non-toxic choice due to their association with health. The old adage, "An apple a day keeps the doctor away," may not be scientifically proven, but it is so ingrained in the cultural consciousness that apple lends great psychic strength to healing rites. A little milk and/or honey adds sweetness and nurturing, and both milk and honey are sacred to Brigid as well. Be sure to use things that you like, and to which you do not have known allergies. Plain water is also fine, but I do strongly encourage putting at least a little bit of salt in the water. Salt is a natural purifier and one that your unconscious mind will connect with purification and healing.

Remember, your journey to the well is a part of the healing process. Treat each step as sacred—even if your journey is simply the walk down the hall to the bathroom.

Some choose to bring an offering to Brigid when making a pilgrimage. Again, apples and dairy products are traditional Brigid offerings, as are whiskey and beer. I have felt fulfilled by bringing her white roses. Food items are good offerings as they break down and don't pollute the land, but a physical offering is not absolutely necessary. While I've left trinkets at sacred wells in Europe, the sanitation department of New York removes things I tie to trees near our water sources and the Hudson River is so full of junk, I feel it wrong to leave anything on the shores that will not biodegrade. Hence, I do not bring an offering every time I make a pilgrimage, but I know many who do. The greatest offering I feel I can give my sacred water sources is to collect garbage when I visit.

Be mindful of animals potentially wandering by the area that might consume food offerings. For instance, do not offer chocolate in an area near a dog park. If you are visiting a well used for drinking, it is best not to empty liquids onto the ground at all. If the well or water source is commonly used for depositing offerings such as coins, you might be all right to also leave an offering yourself. Otherwise, it may be best to leave an offering in a place where it will not fall into the water, such as tying something to a tree branch, or simply leaving an energetic offering, such as prayer or trash collection. It is a good rule of thumb to avoid putting things in the water that do not fall into them at some place naturally. I have on occasion thrown apples into the Hudson River as further upstate, where apples grow naturally, the fruit is likely to fall into the river.

Let your offering ideas come to you naturally, but be mindful as to whether their presence in a public or natural space would cause more harm than good. Mindful action in the area of a well or any other spiritual site is important. Treating a space with reverence and respect keeps the space spiritually sound for all those who may visit in the future. Do not become so invested in your own spiritual experience that you leave unwelcome reminders of your visit (i.e. garbage, or damage to grass or plant life). Tying ribbons or cloth (called *clouties*), or items representative of ailments to be healed, is a common practice at the healing wells of Ireland and the United Kingdom. However, ancient sites such as tombs or stone circles should not be decked with trinkets. A basic rule of thumb: When in doubt, don't. Leaving an energetic offering is certainly acceptable. It lends energy to the space without polluting or tainting it, continually strengthening it as a space of healing for others who may visit.

RITUAL: THE WORK AT THE WELL

This ritual is to better know the nature of Brigid the Well-healer as well as open the door to your own healing path. For some, this working may have profound healing qualities. For others, it will have informative qualities or seal one's commitment to the process of healing.

Get comfortable. If it is safe and acceptable to do so, putting your feet into the water will better connect you to its powers. If you cannot step into the water, sitting or standing in close proximity to the source will do fine. If your well is one you created at home, situate yourself close to or over it. Chant over the water:

Brigid of Water, Brigid of Light
Alleviate me from my plight
Brigid of Water, Brigid of Light
The end of pain is now in sight.

Continue to chant this over and over until you feel the energy start to shift. Some may feel a prickling of their skin and/or their scalp. Others may feel some dizziness, a sense of great joy or peace, or even painful emotions come to the surface. Recognize this as pain leaving your body and psyche. If the tears start flowing, let them. If you feel the need to laugh, do it! Continue to chant and as you do, pay attention to thoughts that arise in your mind or images that come to you. Stay in this space for at least fifteen minutes, setting a timer if need be. Best case scenario, stay as long as you are physically able to do so. You may experience a second energy shift of sorts—possibly a sudden surge of energy, euphoria, or such strong emotions that tears or laughter overtake your chanting. My experience has been an increased sense of peace and heightened awareness.

After your chanting is complete, you may wish to stay in the presence of the well for a time to process what you experienced. When walking away from the well, walk away knowing you are leaving pain behind. Do not turn back or look behind when doing so. This doesn't mean you can't ever return to the well. You can revisit at another time, but for the moment, walk purposefully away from your pain.

If creating a well at home, the same principle applies except that you will want to pour your water down the bath drain, in the yard, or on the street when you have completed it. Turn and do not look back. Some people may choose to bathe as part of their well experience, and this I do think is a healthy and helpful practice, if the herbs contain no known allergens and if it's safe and acceptable to do so.

Do not consume well water unless it comes from a drinking well and you have researched whether it is safe from ground pollutants. Again, back to the basic Well Rule: When in doubt, don't. The basic purpose of this exercise is to release pain, which does not always prove to be compatible with consuming/absorbing. However, if you are able to verify that the water is clean and suitable for drinking and you feel it is essential to your healing practice, good luck and Brigid speed!

Do not forget to offer thanks at the end of your rite. Showing Brigid appreciation for her assistance in the work will strengthen your relationship with her and also contribute energy to a place that assisted you in your healing process.

EXERCISE: THE WELL OF HEART HEALING

Once when Brigid was in Armagh, two persons passed her. They bore a tub of water, as they wished to be blessed by Brigid and healed with the water they brought. The tub fell behind them and went round from the door of the stronghold to a far away lake. They cried out, fearful their tub had broken and water spilled. But it was not broken and not a single drop fell out. Their faith and determination made that Brigid's blessing was upon them and where the water spread, every disease and every ailment in the land was healed.

—Inspired by traditional tale

Reflection: Healing starts with a map, but usually winds through uncharted wilderness. If our plan for healing goes awry, can we trust in Divine Order? Can we be open to a new direction of healing? Can we believe in our own cracked vessels becoming whole?

As a tarot reader and Priestess of Brigid, I often work specifically with heart healing. The healing of the heart is complicated and often trivialized as selfish or unimportant. But hurts we've sustained, caused, or borne witness to leave their own physical or emotional manifestations. In time, the injured heart can become hardened, insensitive, even cruel to others or possibly physically ill, itself. Healing the heart is not selfish. A healed person is more likely to want to heal or help others and often does.

Healing is often represented by gentle images, and wells are often imagined as peaceful. Yet wells are deep and the depths can be murky or dangerous. When we stand at the edge, we cannot see the bottom or what may be in there. Likewise, healing is not always pretty. Healing can be painful, hence why morphine and other pain drugs were invented. Contemporary artists often represent Brigid the Healer as a serene-faced woman, forgetting that Brigid also rules fire and the pressure of the forge.

Many individuals, myself included, have experienced Brigid the Healer as more of a tough physical therapist than a gentle nurse, one focused on the goal of the injured helping themselves to be stronger. The task of emotional healing frequently brings up deep wounds from the darkest wells of our souls. When this happens, it's easy to want to pull back, preferring to exist in familiar illness than take the path of unknown and often uncomfortable healing.

This exercise is designed for your well at home. It can be adapted to your work at a holy well, if you live close to one.

Materials

A piece of lodestone from a local gem dealer, or any dark stone

Salt or Florida Water (also called Agua Florida—easily ordered online, if you don't have a store near you that carries it)

A warm bath or a bowl or basin of water

Place the stone in the water. If you are visiting a body of water or a holy well, bring the stone along but hold it in your hand—do not throw it into the water.

Call to mind the circumstances that pained you. Describe them aloud and envision your words absorbed by the water and the stone. Do not judge the pain or analyze it. Let the anger and the tears fall into the water. When you have said all that you can say, recite the following (adapted from a traditional prayer to St. Brigid for peace):

Brigid, you are a beacon of peace,
Please bring harmony to my conflict,
Light to my darkness,
Hope to my sorrow.
Spread your mantle of peace over my troubles and anxieties.
May my peace be firmly rooted in my heart and world.

Inspire me to act justly, even when justice has not been shown to me.
Brigid, as you are a voice for the wounded and weary,
Strengthen what is wounded and weary in me.
Calm me into a quietness that heals and listens.
May I grow each day into greater wholeness in mind, body, and
   spirit.

At the end of the rite, sit in the space, acknowledging it as a sacred place of healing. Meditate on what you would prefer to see in your world and self, rather than focusing on what you left behind. If you traveled to a well, take the stone with you and throw it over your shoulder before leaving. Do not turn back once you have done so. If you made your well at home, drain the water from the tub or pour the water down the drain. Then, walk to the nearest crossroads or intersection and throw the stone over your shoulder. Do not turn back once you have done so.

EXERCISE: THE WELL OF CLARITY

A good friend of mine was distraught over her young daughter's asthma, which had worsened despite the pediatrician's help. One night, she performed a ritual to Brigid begging for her to heal her daughter. She pleaded to Brigid for a miracle. As she prayed, a thought dawned on her: "Take her to an asthma specialist." With the new thought, she found enough peace to calm herself and her wheezy little girl down to sleep. She made an appointment the next day with a specialist and the girl's condition improved and has continued to improve with the help of the specialist—and Brigid's advice—ever since.

We may want to believe that healing will be a single, power-laced moment and all pain will evaporate with it. In reality, healing is more like an onion—peeling back layers of hurt and blockages until the center of the problem is found, often weeping much of the time. When calling on Brigid the Healer, asking for clarity is often the key. Brigid, being a Goddess of practical tools, is a strong force to call upon when hitting massive blocks to healing and progress, just as in the case of my friend and her daughter.

I've heard stories of Brigid's assistance coming as more of a swift kick than a gentle uplifting. I've witnessed Brigid workers suddenly feeling "pushed" to make drastic lifestyle changes. Toxic people who previously drove these people crazy suddenly vanish from view. Others claim they began despising harmful habits they previously felt they could not live without. I have found that calling on Brigid for help is quite a similar experience to a child calling on their mom for help cleaning their bedroom: tough, direct, and I end up doing most of the work myself, aided by sharp and serious synchronicity. When I call on Brigid for clarity, I prepare for truth to be revealed in a sharp, shrewd fashion. The following exercise is one I developed at a serious block in my career and creative life. While the answer I received was not what I thought I wanted, it was ultimately what I needed.

This exercise is best done at home, unless you are close enough to a natural source of water which you can verify as clean and safe.

To mix a well at home, mix clean water with salt or Florida Water or a combination. The water should have the look of tears. Have a towel ready.

Be present with your blockage. Ask yourself, "What is specifically troubling me at present?" List all details that make up its identity, without judgment, justification, or analysis.

Using a tarot deck, draw a single card. If you have a different divination tool that you prefer, that would be fine as well. If you are not familiar with any divination system, I still encourage the tarot as the images can inform the practitioner greatly. Most tarot decks come with a book of the meanings of the cards. However, the most authentic messages come from the first internal responses you have when looking at the tarot. This card is meant to represent you and where you are in your journey at that moment. Draw a second card to lay over it, the cards will form a "T" shape. The second card represents what is truly blocking your progress. Allow your first thoughts to inform you about the nature of the situation.

Leaning over the water, chant the following:

Brigid of Power, Brigid of Light,
Help me see into my plight.

Continue to chant until the chant takes up more space in your mind than the problem at hand. When you feel the chant has done its job, close your eyes tightly and wash your face with the water. Particularly take time to wipe over your eyelids, as in removing that which blocks your sight, but also take care so as not to get the water directly into your eyes. Take note of thoughts or feelings that arise as you do this.

After doing this a few times, pat your face and eyes dry with the towel before opening them. Once you've opened your eyes again, draw a third tarot card. The third card is meant to represent tools to break the blockage or a new focus. Take note of what you've seen and experienced.

Discard the water in the garden, yard, or at an intersection. When you've thrown the water out, turn and walk away from it and do not look back.

When It Doesn't Seem to Work . . .

Sometimes, well seekers may not see or feel anything after the work is complete. This may mean that they're not ready to be healed, or it may be that the practice or well is not the right fit for them. It could also mean that the healing is to come in the days ahead. I have seen and experienced many situations where a specific ritual or rite did not seem effective in the moment, but later found that it actually had worked. If you do not feel a difference in the days after your healing rite, you may want to try it again on another day. Allow the changes to manifest on their own schedule, not impeded by expectation or an artificial timeline. If nothing manifests after a second try, you might want to try a different well or a different practice altogether.

Some ailments can't be cured by medication or by spiritual means. Some ailments can't be cured at all. This is a painful truth to human existence. But humans are creatures who try. To not attempt to repair or heal when options are still available is counterintuitive to our nature as a species. The attempt of healing, whether successful or not, teaches us about the nature of healing itself, perhaps developing tools for future needs. Brigid, in her role as the Well Keeper, inspires the cultivation of healing through drive, journey, and providence. But to know this aspect of Brigid, we must start by digging to the source of our own wells. Wells need tending. They can become overgrown with brush, polluted by contaminants, or paved over and forgotten completely until time, luck, and hard work restore them. Likewise, our own souls need the same care. We must dig through pain, bad habits, resentment, fear, and a laundry list of other soul-cloggers to find our own wellspring of healing. Brigid work requires the diligence one would need to apply to the restoration of a physical well. Let her be your guide in discovering your own path to healing. It won't be tidy or easy, but it will be complete and you will not be alone on any step of the way.

CHAPTER 4

Brigid the Bard: Goddess of the Arts and Craftsmanship

Adjuva Brigitta!

O Brigid Help Me!

—Phrase found on ancient manuscripts of Irish

scribes

I once had a science teacher who believed music was developed when humans tried to replicate the sounds of animals and weather. Art, music, and story originally expressed human experience of the confusing mysteries of existence. Art connects us to our collective past and, in a way, connects us to future generations we may never meet yet who will hopefully enjoy the same creations we love today. The arts are the voice of the Gods themselves. In many of her myths, Brigid is often called "the Poet." But in the world of the ancient Celts, poetry meant more than pleasant sounding words in rhythmic order. Poetry, and the arts, was the mystical work of the Celtic Bard. The Celtic Bards formulated the wonder and mystery of the complicated world into a palatable form through poetry, story, and music. Some interpretations list Brigid as first and foremost a Goddess of Bards and all of her other aspects—including healing—being secondary.

During a massive research trip for this book, I found that water and fire remained consistent symbols among Brigid images, while her other attributes varied through the different regions. In seaside or fishing communities, Brigid is a protector of fisherman. In the small village of Chelvey, England, which is a farming community, there is a 900-year-old church dedicated to St. Bridget. The altar cloths of are decorated with wheat. The churchwarden's wife mentioned bread as a primary area of Brigid patronage. I asked her to elaborate as I had heard stories of cheese and milk being sacred to Brigid, but not bread.

"It's the end product," she replied.

The idea was craftsmanship. Brigid the Bard as the Patroness of poetry and song is not the full picture. Rather, like the Bardic process, it's the power of the end product that exemplifies Brigid as a Goddess of Bardic Arts.

CELTIC BARDS: SAGES AND MAGES

The term *Bard* referred to a person of the highest education of their time, instructed in storytelling, and music. Bards may have been a subset of the Druid caste. While the Druids are frequently credited with mysticism, religion, and magick, they also worked extensively with science and mathematics, with quite a sophisticated understanding of both. Pomponius Mela, another writer from ancient Greece, wrote of the Druids' talents with the most complex problems in geometry, among others. A subset of such a learned group would certainly have had an equally complex understanding of the structures of music or worded work, which relies on mathematics as well. Bards are typically imagined as having several areas of expertise. They worked with the ability to arrange words in a way that gave them increased magickal potency when spoken. Perhaps even more importantly, the

Bards kept the oracular history and teachings of the Druids. Both of these abilities were so important to the Celtic culture that Romans were known to cut out the tongues of Druidic Bards as a measure of taking power in the region. The ability to use and understand language in such a magickal way was considered a gift from Brigid.

While the absence of written lore can be sometimes frustrating for lovers of Celtic history, oracular tradition was a deliberate choice. Caesar recorded that Druids learned and taught by memorized verse. It was possibly considered "unlawful" to write things down, the idea being that memorization strengthened the overall mind, a sentiment with which Caesar himself agreed. Unfortunately for us, this means much of what the Druids practiced and studied will remain a permanent mystery. But the Bardic spirit was never fully extinguished. It has persevered and preserved the sense of spirit and magick in a more profound way than written word ever could.

Music was integral to ancient Celtic life. Each house was said to have one or more harps, and young women were taught to play, continuously keeping music within the house from dawn to dusk. Music and lore told around the fireside were believed integral to the health of the home. The other two primary instruments were the pipe and the *crwth*, a type of violin, both common in Wales in particular.

Crwth.

The Celts were renowned for their extraordinary musical talent, said to "Always begin with B-flat and return to same, the music designed to be beautiful and pleasing and continuous." The Bards were endowed with faculty for rhymed speeches said to be subtle and ingenious, producing stories as ornaments of wonderful and exquisite invention, both in words and sentences. The *file*, the Bard for the Royal Court, was expected to know 350 great poems of adventures, cattle raids, feasts, battles, elopements, slaughters, visions, loves, expeditions, invasions, caves, voyages, sieges, births, and frenzies so that one could be recited on every night of the year save for fifteen feast days which required other entertainment. These stories included the movements of celestial bodies, seasons, and storms—things the Druids certainly would have consulted. Pieces eventually recorded by either Christian monastics or even penned by the Bards who joined the monasteries themselves remain the best sources of insight into Celtic mythology, beliefs, and practices. Perhaps even seeing the value of the work, some of the saints, St. Columba being one, worked against the later oppression of Bardic traditions by the Church.

Religiously speaking, the Bards played key roles in the celebration of Druidic holidays. Through their oral history, Bards are thought to have helped Druids build their calendars. Bards may have also acted as prophets themselves periodically, possibly working themselves into frenzy from music and chant so as to invoke prophetic moments. This was described as a violent roaring, a stark diversion from the common thought that Bards had a solely lyrical, fluid practice. As the prophets and tale-spinners of the Druid caste, the Bards also had a likely hand in spellcraft, invoking divine messages for ways to avert dangerous forces, such as storms and illnesses.

The magickal importance of poetry, story, and song is illustrated in Celtic myth and legends. Heroes often got out of tricky situations by enchanting Kings, Gods, and Goddesses with song and poetry. One myth tells of a man who could not find his wife, but came upon her one magickal night, years after she vanished, nursing a fairy baby on a *sidhe* mound, where the fairies lived and kept her, singing to her husband to show him how to break the spell. Music, poetry, and storytelling are mythic tools of seduction, but also of protection. Songs and song-makers were so important that they appear to alleviate their makers of legal fault, and gave the Bards a place of privilege. Bards received clothing from the King and the Queen, free land, and a horse. They were placed next to the captain of guard in the great halls with harp in hand and always available to sing, recite verse, or tell a story on the King or Queen's command. Bards would travel to court and sing praises of the generous hospitality of the host, the bravery of battle, and laments for the lost kin.

The idea of the Bard is one of the craftsperson. It was necessary that Bards excel in numerous areas—not just a single instrument. The trade was learned through discipleship under an older or superior Bard, who taught not just poetry and music, but the explicit use of words, history, folklore, legends, genealogy, and history. When traveling, the Bard was expected to entertain his patron, praise his virtues, memorize his lineage, and also recite works of earlier Bards. Every bit of this was learned and performed through intense memorization.

Bardism in its original form suffered beginning with the onset of Christianity, to the late Middle Ages for its "Pagan" nature. Under the command of the Church, the magick and ritual disappeared, but the music and stories continued to flourish in the great halls and villages. The *Seanchaí*, the storyteller, held immense respect in communities. In Leon Uris's *Trinity,* the main character apologizes profusely to the local *Seanchaí* for inadvertently comparing him to a "lowly Catholic priest." A woman *Seanchaí* often sang or chanted stories reminiscent of the era of Bards.

Bardism suffered not only from Christian suppression, but also from the Great Famine and emigration. Even so, Ireland maintained renown for an immense number of poets and writers, in an extremely high density for such a physically small country. Today, the practice of sharing song and story is so very ingrained into the culture that many individuals may not even realize they are filling the role of the ancient Bards, the work being as natural as breathing. In places I've traveled, everyone has their "party piece," the story or song they are expected to tell at a gathering. I've been lovingly reprimanded several times at Irish gatherings for not having a proper piece prepared. Even in Celtic Christianity, Irish prayers are known for brevity so they can easily be recited without a book, possibly yet another link to the Bardic ancestry. A genuine resurgence of Bards in the formal sense continues to grow. The practice is expanding from the living room and fireside into a cultural mainline in the urban paradigm. Even the Irish passport carries a harp as its emblem.

Each of the four Irish provinces (some say five, the fifth being a mystical province not of this Earth) had its own tutelary Goddess who was responsible for legal and ritual dominion in that region. Brigid's province was Leinster, located on the southeastern side of Ireland. The official sigil of Leinster features a harp as its central image. It stands to wonder if Leinster was known for being a particularly artistic province, and that Brigid was believed to bless its inhabitants with the power of song and story. While many myths describe her as "Brigid the Poet," such as bringing poetry to the world when she arrived alongside the

Dagda's other children, Brigid cannot be readily found championing Bardic arts in her myths in the way she forcefully invokes healing in others. The ability to use verse and song as a method of protection and clever action was frequently handed off to other heroes, but perhaps Brigid served as the source of inspiration.

> *Lugh, the Shining One, approached the house of the Tuatha Dé Danann and asked to be received. "You cannot enter," the porter said, "unless you have a talent matched by none beneath this roof." "I am a master of smithworking and warriorship," said Lugh. "We have Goibnu the Smith and Ogma the Warrior. We have no need of you," the porter replied. "I am a harpist," said Lugh. "We already have a harpist and a fine one too," said the porter. "We have no need of you ..."*
>
> —INSPIRED BY TRADITIONAL TALE

Brigid is not mentioned in this myth, but her siblings are. Goibnu is credited with her usual domain of smithworking, but no name is given to the harpist. As the harpist of the home was most often a woman, we could assume a Divine female kept the music going in the Great Hall of the Gods. Perhaps this is where Brigid quietly enters the space as Bard.

Reflection: Not everyone is a poet or a singer. The good news is that we don't have to be either. Where do our talents shine? Where do they blend into one another? In the manner that the songs and stories of the Bards also acted as charms and incantations, what power might our own work have? Can we communicate change? Can we inspire peace? Do we motivate action? How far might your work stretch? Imagine for a moment that every talent you own, no matter the level of glamour, expertise, or anonymity impacts the whole world. How does it? Like Brigid in the story, do your talents ever become overshadowed by others? How do we maintain our work in a world of fierce competition? How can we make our voices count? Do we need to be recognized for the work to be effective?

THE END PRODUCT

Stories of Brigid focus extensively on milk production. One of many tales of her as saint is laced with quite prominent Pagan overtones, telling of the infant St. Brigid vomiting up any food that was "impure," but growing up strong and powerful on the milk of a white cow with red ears. The white cow with red ears is a link to the Otherworld, but milk products suggest elements of Bardic work to them as well. The production of cheese takes skill and time. It's curious to wonder if Brigid's consumption of Otherwordly milk is a parable of divine inspiration; "being fed by" a greater source to complete a product of great worth and value. It was the mystery and gift of inspiration which seemed to come from elsewhere. St. Brigid is known as a Patroness of beer. The brew, like the other Bardic arts, takes great time and craftsmanship. In fact, Brigid's abilities with beer were *so* profound, it is said that she could change water into beer. The following prayer to St. Brigid reveals her importance in Celtic Christianity by giving her talents similar to Jesus Christ, who turned water into wine:

I should like a great lake of beer to give to God.
I should like the angels of Heaven to be tippling there for all
*   eternity.*
I should like the men of Heaven to live with me, to dance
*   and sing.*
If they wanted I'd put at their disposal vats of suffering.
White cups of love I'd give them with a heart and a half.
Sweet pitchers of mercy I'd offer to every man.
I'd make Heaven a cheerful spot,

Because the happy heart is true.

I'd make men happy for their own sakes.

I should like Jesus to be there too.

I'd like the people of Heaven to gather from all the parishes
    around.

I'd give a special welcome to the women,

The three Marys of great renown.

I'd sit with the men, the women of God,

There by the great lake of beer

We'd be drinking good health forever,

And every drop would be a prayer.

— TRADITIONAL

BARDIC TASKS OF THE SOUL

Brigid's miraculous works and tremendous charity drew the attention of St. Brendan, who came to visit her at Kildare. When he arrived, she greeted him in the fields where she had been working and invited him into her house for tea. As it had been a rainy day, she wore a rain cloak. Once inside the house, she flung off her cloak without bothering to hang it up. There was no need, as the cloak hung upon a sunbeam streaming through the window like a cloth on an oak limb. St. Brendan, astounded by the sight, tried to fling his own wet cloak over the same sunbeam and became frustrated when it repeatedly fell to the floor. "Never worry," said Brigid to her new friend. "I've only been practicing it longer. It comes with time."

—INSPIRED BY TRADITIONAL TALE

The Celts and their Bards understood that the work of solid craft took many years and immense focus. This energy hasn't left the Bardic aspect of Brigid, yet this may be one of the tougher lessons for contemporary practitioners. Overnight fame, the exuberance over prodigies, the idea of "You either have it, or you don't," is the normal thought mode, at least in the United States (although I don't think this is unique to Americans). One reason why this is my first published book is because I bought too deeply into the idea that if I wasn't perfect at anything the first time I tried it, it wasn't worth doing at all. I didn't understand that writing, like music or painting or even developing computer code, takes patience, skill, and practice. This book was a huge lesson in Bardic Brigid. What started with what felt like divine inspiration direct from Brigid herself was followed by several years of research, false starts, travel, questions, confusion, and much hair pulling before I had something that looked like a final product worthy of production.

> One day as Brigid rode out and about from one engagement to another, the charioteer realized the Lady would be late. Instead of taking the circuitous path, he decided to cut through the field to save a bit of time. As they bounced along, the wheel of the chariot hit a hole. The axle broke and the Beloved Lady went flying out of the chariot, muddying herself. The charioteer, abjectly horrified, helped Brigid to her feet and offered the most profuse apologies heard in this world, the next or the next. Brigid smiled and dusted the grass and dung from her cloak. "Lesson learned, my son," said Brigid. "Shortcuts lead to long delays."
>
> —INSPIRED BY TRADITIONAL TALE

Reflection: What is worth the journey? What is worth the work? Is the interest only in the end product? Is there interest in the journey as well? Would we still take the journey, knowing there could be a risk of no end product? Can we accept that risk? Can we be willing to take our time?

WORKING WITH BRIGID THE BARD

If you are attracted to the Bardic aspect of Brigid, don't be frightened off by my doleful tales! The idea of the long journey is that it ultimately means the end product will be all that much stronger. Brigid the Bard loves to help those who create. Musicians, artists, performers, and writers have a great deal of success with Brigid's creator magick, but they are not the only ones to benefit. Engineers, drawing from Brigid's Smithworker blessings of innovation, would be prime beneficiaries of Bardic spellwork. I have also seen chefs, teachers, entrepreneurs, and other developers connect well with Brigid the Bard.

In short, looking to Brigid for a quick fix is a naught notion. That being the case, those who look to Brigid for inspiration may be disappointed when their desires manifest as long, drawn-out projects that take years, and not a single fervent burst of effortless outcome. Go to Brigid for inspiration, but expect that it will come with work aplenty and endurance tests of patience. While the Bard is something of an idealized character, it embodies that which must be sought, honed, and honed again. If one is not driven or patient enough, the spirit of the Bard will not shine through. Yet, using Brigid in your work of the arts, craftsmanship, or any endeavor that requires honing and patience, will provide you the support required to complete it.

The legacy of the Bard is more than music or culture, although those things can very much stand alone in their importance. Of the tools that Brigid brought to world, the work of the Bard provides a special kind of profound resonance. All were necessary for survival, but the Bards gave meaning, order, and preservation to these worlds. Viewed in that light, the idea of Brigid as an unending well, perpetual flame, and providence of song and poetry make sense. All endure. All preserve. Anyone whose heart has ever leapt at the sound of an old song, or been wrenched by a classic work of writing can testify to the timeless power of art. Our contemporary view of the Well might be a bottle of vitamins and the Forge might be industry and, without underestimating the importance of either, it's the work of the Bard that shapes our memories. Tastes and trends may change with the frequency of oceanic tides, yet Brigid stands as guardian over the parts of human expression that withstand taste and trend—finding commonalities with the previous, the present, and the future even as the generations progress.

The following rituals are written for individuals to perform alone. However, they can easily be augmented to include a working partner or other people. As with any ritual, use these instructions as guidelines—*especially* when doing magick for creative inspiration. Should you feel creatively inspired to do something other than what you see below, follow that! It makes no sense to stick to the book and stifle creativity when doing work for creativity.

SPELL: TO RECEIVE INSPIRATION FROM BRIGID THE BARD

Materials

A candle: suggested colors red, white, or gold/yellow. For a small creative spark, use a tea light, a votive, or a small two-hour taper candle, which can be found at most occult stores. For major inspiration, use a seven-day or pull-out jar candle, which can also generally be found at your local or online occult store.

A small bowl or cup of earth or salt.

A small bowl or cup of clean water. You have to drink it! Don't add things to it!

If you have a trade or passion, consider carving symbols that represent it into your candle: music notes, a paintbrush, or even a symbol of your nation's currency if you would like to bring creative income. Take liberties with bringing items related to what you would like the Bardic energies to touch into your magick space: art supplies, sheet music, business cards, crochet needles or patterns, and so forth. If all of these suit you, bring them all! Again, the Bards held multiple roles and so can you (unless you're like me and have to focus on *focus* rather than diversity). If you are without a specific craft or trade, go in with nothing and be open to anything. In either case, also consider carving your name into the candle and don't hesitate to, using your fingers, dab a bit of your saliva on the candle wick. Your DNA will pick up the energies you create and better infuse the spell.

Set your space, be it your Magick Space (please see Chapter 10 on Brigid Magick for more information and examples), or just some time behind the locked bathroom door. Burning sage or a pleasant incense will help settle the energies of the room. If you don't have or don't want to use those things, a few deep breaths will set the tone of the room beautifully.

When you are ready, light the candle and say aloud or focus on the phrase, *"I light the flame of inspiration."*

With fingers pointed as a triangle at your heart (see image below), position yourself so it would make sense that the flame energy could literally enter through the finger-portal. Say aloud or chant internally the following, *"Adjuva Brigitta! Adjuva Brigitta! Inspire my heart! Inspire my soul! Adjuva Brigitta! Adjuva Brigitta! Inspire my heart! Inspire my soul!"* Repeat the phrase as you envision the flame's energy entering your heart and pulsing through your body with each beat, filling each capillary and cell with the power of Bardic Inspiration. When you feel the energy has reached its peak, release your hands and stop the chant.

Example of setting and hand position.

Next, take the bowl of earth or salt. Tap the bowl or the earth particles in a rhythmic sense. Say aloud, *"Adjuva Brigitta! Adjuva Brigitta! Inspire my patience! Inspire my strength! Adjuva Brigitta! Adjuva Brigitta! Inspire my patience! Inspire my strength!"* Continue the chant and the tapping until you can envision the very words tapping on your heart and soul. When you feel the energy has reached its peak, stop the tapping and set down the bowl.

Finally, take the cup or bowl of water. Gently rotating the bowl in a circular way so that the water moves but does not slosh, say aloud, *"Adjuva Brigitta! Adjuva Brigitta! Brigid flow through me! Brigid flow through me! Adjuva Brigitta! Adjuva Brigitta! Brigid flow through me! Brigid flow through me!"* When you feel the energy has reached its peak, drink the water—all of it— and set down the bowl.

For the last part of the rite, take a series of deep breaths, allowing the air to settle the energy you've just raised. If you have a goal in mind for Bardic Brigid's help, focus on that. If you don't yet have your creative aspirations identified, now is a good time to allow potential visions of that aspiration to come to mind. It may come instantly, or it may emerge in the days to come.

The rite has closed. In honor of the spirit of Bardic Brigid, setting out an open bottle of beer or a cup of tea in your sacred space is appropriate, but not required. You can also entertain Brigid with a song or art piece of your own making, or by reading something written for her by someone else, such as one of the pieces in this book. If you leave a libation, pouring it out later in the yard, garden, or in a nearby park is a good way to return the energy to the source.

Natural to the work of the Bard, do not expect quick results and plan to take time. This ritual should be a jumping off point for your relationship with Bardic Brigid. You may walk out with bursts of inspiration and if you do, that's great! But if you don't, the rite is not a failure. Be open to ideas and opportunities as they present themselves in the coming weeks after doing this. You'll probably find yourself far more flooded with ideas than you ever thought possible.

SPELL: TO BREAK A PARTICULARLY NASTY CREATIVE BLOCK

Sometimes a creative block is a project's way of saying, "I need a nap before I can function properly." However, if the creative block is happening for an alarmingly long time or if your livelihood is dependent on it giving way, here's a practice to help it along.

Take a metal baking dish (it must be metal) and fill it with water and a small portion of milk. As you are doing this, tell the milk and the water your troubles. This may sound odd if you're new to magick work, but try to envision that the water will be affected by emotions and influence. Take the pan and stick it in your freezer. Give it several hours as it needs to be frozen solid.

When the water and milk have frozen into brick form, make a large cup of tea. If you're really blocked, consider boiling a whole pot of water and steeping several tea bags in it.

Take the block to the threshold of your home or building. Make sure you are over concrete or stone. If your home threshold could be damaged by a chunk of ice being hurled at it, better to use the curb.

Hurl the pan, ice-side down, onto the threshold or curb and cry out or scream in your head, *"ADJUVA BRIGITTA! BRIGID BREAK THE BLOCK!"*

Pour the hot tea over the ice pieces. Know that as the ice melts, so does your block.

Remember to thank Brigid in your intentions when the creative juices begin flowing again.

Worried about what the neighbors will think? Hey, I live in New York City and do this kind of stuff and no one seems to think a thing, but maybe it's because I live in NYC and people don't pay much attention. But what is more important? Breaking your creative block or hiding your eccentricities from the neighbors? If you're an eccentric magick worker, chances are good the neighbors won't be surprised to see you yell at pieces of ice in front of your house.

RITUAL: RECEIVING BARDIC DIRECTION FOR YOUR WORK

If you'd like some assistance from Brigid the Bard regarding what steps to take next for your work, the following practice may prove helpful.

Mix water with a touch of honey and, if willing, a touch of beer as well. (The beer is optional, but the honey is important if you are not allergic to it as it is the end-product of the bees' work.

Agave may be used as a substitute if needed.) Sprinkle the mixture three times around the space where you will be doing the rite. If you have a creative space or workspace, such as a studio or office, that would be a good setting to do this work. As always, light a candle in honor of Brigid's enduring flame. Knock three times on the doorway of the space. Say the following:

Depth of Well,
Bright of Flame,
Brigid hear me call Your name,
Guide my words, my work, my art,
Shine Your light into my dark.

Repeat the verse aloud or in your head until the words seem to blur together. Focus on what information you need. Imagine a brilliant light into every crevice of shadow within your mind, heart, or wherever you feel your creative source springs. If you use tarot, runes, or crystals, or any other sort of divinatory device, now is the time to consult them. If you do not, simply sit in the space for a time and see what images come to you. Whether a clear message comes or not (sometimes the work is not instantaneous), keep an eye for omens in the coming days in relation to your work.

The rite will end when you extinguish the candle.

To invoke the Bard into prophetic dreams, sprinkle the water used in the rite on your bed and pillow. Rub on to your temples for extra effect—but *not* if you have honey allergies! Dreams influenced by Brigid the Bard may then help you finish work you have begun or show you better ways to complete it.

CHAPTER 5

The Forge and the Anvil: Brigid the Fire Goddess

Hail reign a fair maid with gold upon your toe
Open up the West Gate and let the Old Year go;
Hail reign a fair maid with gold upon your chin,
Open up the East Gate and let the New Year in;
Levideu sing Levideu the water and the wine,
The seven bright gold wires and candles that do shine.

—FROM TRADITIONAL WELSH, said at Candlemas (Imbolc)

rites

The tri-fold identity of Brigid is interdependent. Healing needs the power of fire to burn away impurities, artistic inspiration requires the beauty of the well or natural water. The third face of Brigid, alongside her images of pouring water or singing song, finds her pounding on a forge. This is Brigid the Smith. The smith needs water to temper the steel after it has been forged, but also needs the Bardic spirit to inspire the shape of the work to be done on the forge. Brigid is a guardian of each of these distinct areas, but perhaps her most important guardianship is in where they all meet.

Fire is pure. Air and water may become polluted and earth can become barren, but fire cannot be tainted and still exist. Its vulnerability is distinct from its elemental counterparts in that only fire can be extinguished in an instant, whereas the others cannot. For the Celts, fire was an immaterial, immortal mystery. Its presence was dangerous and yet vital to the technology that would launch and support their civilization. Fire demanded the same reverence of water and the arts and was yet another jurisdiction of Brigid.

BRIGID OF THE SUN

Reverence for fire likely originated in reverence for the sun. The four major Celtic holidays were aligned with the sun's annual patterns, in honor of their link to the agricultural cycles. The primordial fire of the sun, whose influence was vital to crop fertility and food production, was seen as a miraculous entity. As was the case with many natural phenomena, the Celts had not one God or Goddess of the sun, but several. They also worshipped Gods who were more associated with the uses of these natural phenomena than being actual Deities of it. In Britain, where Brig was called Brigantia, she was probably not considered a Goddess who bore the identity of the sun itself, yet in her later carved depictions, she wore a crown that looked very much like. After their arrival in Britain, the Romans linked Brigantia to their own sun Goddess Sulis, in addition to Minerva. In these guises, Brigantia is a not only a purveyor of the sun's bounty, but an actual embodiment of the celestial body. The Earth's foliage transmutes the energy of the sun into flora and fauna. A Goddess of the land would not be far removed from the image of the sun. Brigid was said to shoot flame from her skull, possibly a very old image as indicated in her British-Brigantia face, with the flaming sun-crown.

*The eternal flame of Brigid on the cross on the altar at
St. Bridget's Church at St. Bride's Bay, Wales.*

CELTIC FIRE WORSHIP AND REVERENCE

Fire worship was a cornerstone of Celtic practice and perpetual fires were kept on Druidic altars and in places of worship. As lovely as this image may seem, Druidic fire worship wasn't necessarily pretty. Some Druidic rites are thought to have included a giant, man-shaped contraption made of wicker. The legendary and infamous "Wicker Man" was supposedly stuffed with live animals and people, set afire to honor a Celtic Sun God named *Bealtaine*, encouraging the fertility of the soil in the early days of May.

According to their Roman contemporaries, the Druids supposedly watched the death throes of the sacrificed humans and animals for divinatory signs about the temperament of the Gods and how they might be appeased. Roman explorers wrote about the practice in panicked detail, likely because their own captured soldiers were a favored sacrificial choice. In the next chapter, we will look closer at these practices, but in the meantime, questions about the Wicker Man have furrowed brows of historians and archeologists for ages. How did such a giant structure stay upright? How did so much burn so efficiently in an area of the world and time of the year known for abundant dampness? Ancient writers did not leave these answers in their stories, and yet the lore is firmly entrenched into collective consciousness. However it was revered, fire had power. Flame held mystery. This naturally dangerous yet profoundly beneficial element that came from mysterious sparks or bolts of lightning from the Gods left an indelible imprint on Celtic religious practice. Fire was the ultimate sacrifice and a direct connection with the Divine. Through this proverbial burning gate, humanity could reach the immortal. Perhaps remnants of this relationship with fire inspire the candles that light churches, temples, and altars around the world both within and outside the Celtic legacy.

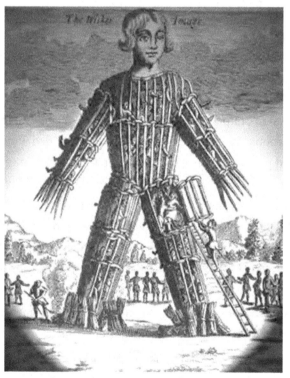

A drawing of the legendary "Wicker Man."

BRIGID AS FIRE GODDESS

In folklore, the name Brigid is often synonymous with "fiery arrow," "bright arrow," or "the bright one," although the modern etymology points to the root "Brig" simply meaning "exalted" or "Brigid" meaning simply "Lady." Whether or not the nicknames are linguistically accurate, they are certainly descriptive of Brigid's personality. "Fiery arrow" is a regularly used nickname for Brigid, conveying the flame that she is known for or perhaps as an analogy for the rays of the sun. Spiritually, Brigid's fiery arrows are summoned for direction and striking the heart of the situation. The fiery aspect of Brigid encompasses swift change, powerful manifestations, and a kind of spiritual internal combustion necessary for completion, drive, and inspiration.

Glimpses of Brigid as Fire Goddess are easily recognized in her incarnation as St. Brigid. One myth of the child saint describes a time when the house in which she lived in appeared to be on fire. The neighbors rushed to extinguish the flames, but on arrival found that there was no fire at all. They concluded that Brigid was filled with the Holy Spirit, a kind of spiritual fire that empowered without destruction.

If water is both life's beginning and the salve after the wound is suffered (as well as the tempering of the hot iron after the forge), and the Bard is the inspiration for the creation, the sun and Brigid's connection to fire holds the space between the beginning and completion. In reflecting on Brigid as the sun, it is more reflection on the rays than on the heavenly body. The rays are the physical connection from the source to the need and it is in the rays where Brigid is connected to the sun, as seen in the story of hanging her cloak on the sunbeam told in the previous chapter. Likewise, Brigid the Fire Goddess connects us from where we begin and where we hope or need to go. Best of all, the flame is perpetual.

*St. Brigid portrait, holding perpetual flame, at the
Church of St. Bridget, Dyserth, Wales.*

Without a doubt, Brigid's most famous flame can be found
in the village of Kildare, located in the province of Leinster.
There, a shrine to St. Brigid holds the perpetually burning flame.
The area is believed to have originated as a Pagan shrine and
the original flame tended by nineteen Druidesses. This was a
place that supposedly never admitted men into its sanctuary
and the perpetual flame never produced ash. The sanctuary was
tended by virgin Priestesses and the leader was always called
Brigid, but likely in a form as *The Brigid,* indicating her leadership role more so than her name. The idea of virgin Priestesses
did not necessarily mean that these women spent their entire
lives without ever knowing sexual experiences. Rather, they did
not associate regularly with men so that their entire lives could
be devoted to supporting the shrine, which was believed to promote the fertility of the land, rather than divert their energies to
pregnancy and child-rearing. Any children born to these women
were likely sent off for fostering by other women in the region.
Nineteen Priestesses tended the perpetual fire, the number possibly correlating with the nineteen-year cycle of the Celtic "great

year." Each Priestess would take a night to sit with the fire and tend it. On the twentieth night, the fire would be left for the Goddess to tend by herself. The nineteenth Priestess would say to the shrine, "Brigid, charge your own fire for this night belongs to you." When the area became Christianized, the tradition continued, with nineteen nuns watching the flame. On the twentieth night, the flame was left alone for St. Brigid to tend. "Brigid, tend your flame," the nineteenth nun would say. "For the twentieth night is yours."

The shrine at Kildare, believed to be the original location of the perpetual fire. This is now a site of pilgrimage at St. Brigid's Church in Kildare, Ireland. Photo courtesy of Elizabeth Guerra-Walker.

The practice at Kildare continued up until the Reformation when it, along with many Catholic practices, were suppressed for their decidedly Pagan elements. A shrine for the original fire temple exists where the original was believed to be and in the late twentieth century, the Brigid flame was relit by the modern day Brigidine Sisters in Kildare and a monument to the perpetual flame was erected in the town square. While the temple remains a point of pilgrimage for lovers of Brigid, the flame itself is kept in a nearby cottage and tended by the local Brigidine Sisters, an order of nuns devoted to St. Brigid.

If her sacred fires at Kildare are a clue to the Goddess's mysteries, they certainly encompass endurance and eternal legacy. Brigid has been associated with other Goddesses, such as the Hindu Kali or the Egyptian Sekhmet, for their associations with sun and fire. But unlike these other fire Goddesses, Brigid's fire represents the product of fire rather than consumption or destruction by it. While there is certainly a place and need for destruction by fire (forests rely on periodic burnings for their health), this is not the role of Brigid's flame. Perhaps this is why the Kildare flame was said to have never extinguished or created ashes. If ash is what remains when other things are consumed, Brigid's ash-less fire reminds us that progress and growth does not have to be dependent on consumption and destruction. Perhaps a better Brigid fire symbol than even the legendary Wicker Man fires could be the burning candle on the writing table, the flame in the lantern, or the fire in the hearth. Other modern equivalents might include the furnace or boiler. It is in this sentiment that the world needs Brigid's fire—and sun—more than ever. The Chelvey cathedral dedicated to St. Brigid is nearly a thousand years old and, at the time of this book, has yet to build a bathroom facility, but it is entirely powered by solar panels—a contemporary manifestation of Brigid's direction of the power of fire into production without destruction.

Reflection: Brigid's fire is akin to the soul's internal fire—what we crave, what we desire, what we must endure. As the flame that never dies or destroys, Brigid fire motivates and leads. Seeking Brigid's fire is a journey not only to manifest our deepest desires, it calls us to question what kind of legacy we want to leave. As in a symbolic act of burning our names into permanent structures, what image will our names leave behind? Brigid's Water Mysteries may be about knowing and healing the Self and her Bardic Mysteries express the Self, but the Fire Mysteries extend beyond the Self. No act for the Self can embody the Spirit of Brigid if it leaves nothing for those who will never know your own Self. What flames can we light that will continue our legacy? What ideas can we inspire that will stimulate long after our names have been forgotten? It's a daunting idea, but like the flame of Kildare that endures in a tiny candle, so can the tiniest, simplest motions set today endure forever.

BRIGID: THE SMITH

The Fire face of Brigid is depicted as the Smithworker. In our contemporary world, few people have much (if any) access to a blacksmith's shop. Industry and invention may have removed the smith trade from its previous role as the central technological turbine of industry, but in Brigid's early days, the smith's work was of fundamental importance. The importance of iron in the ancient Celtic world cannot be underestimated. The only remote comparison we may be able to wrap our heads around is the development of the computer and its effect on the world, but it still doesn't quite do it justice. The development of work with iron ore literally launched the Celts' entire civilization from a collection of scattered tribes to the major economic and culture force of its time. The process of smithworking originated in the Far East, but the natural abundance of iron ore in the Celtic area of Europe made it possible for this technology to grow and boost an entire world from its bellows and anvil. While the Celts remained eclectic even after its development, iron was a main unifying factor in the Celtic world—essentially, what made the Celts into the Celts. The new technology allowed advanced transportation through chariots, and better weaponry through swords and axes. These tools allowed the Celts to engage in trade and provided advantages in warfare, which included pillaging and plundering their Roman neighbors. These things certainly had economic advantages and made for a prosperous Celtic world. Iron was more than a tool. It was a new way of living.

The smithy was a centerpiece of social and cultural activity. Generally located in the center of a settlement, town, or village, patrons would bring their tools for mending, along with orders for nails or other instruments of work. The smithy was a general hub for information or news. This is true even today. As part of my research for this book, I paid a visit to a smithy in East Hampton, New York. As the smith carried on his work, locals came by to say hello, share some gossip, or trade a few stories from about town.

Smithworkers served a function for the Celts beyond the practical wielding and shaping of iron. When I visited the blacksmith shop, an older man walked in and said, "If I could only have one guy on my team, it would be a blacksmith. A blacksmith can do it all." Even in the twenty-first century, the role of the smith is an honored one. A few thousand years ago, iron's invaluable contributions were seen as divine and its maker held a role equal to that of a magician.

The work cultivated an aura of otherworldly power. The smith transformed seemingly useless metallic ore into something extremely powerful and useful, an item not found naturally. The smithy stayed dimly lit so that the smith could best see the colors of the metal and the fire change, which would define when it was time to strike and shape the iron. The dark environment gave their shop another world of mystery. Smiths guarded the secrets of their work carefully, mostly to avert potential competition. To learn the secrets of smithing, one began as a child—sweeping the floor and tending to the needs of shop. The process from apprentice to journeyman to master required decades, akin to the study the Druids required for their own mastery. In the darkened room where the fires and bellows blow green smoke, the prism of blue, gold, and white flame, and the astounding transformation of the raw, cold iron into strong, usable material, it is easy to see why the smith was viewed as a magick worker.

Iron even had a role of particular significance in averting evil spirits, possibly harking back to an even earlier time when the iron-wielding Celts overtook their bronze-age peers. Iron found its way into brooches, pins, and amulets. Women in childbirth safeguarded their laboring space with a row of nails or an iron reaping hook so that evil spirits would not approach them or their infants.

Although smithworking is traditionally work performed by men due to its reliance on upper-body strength, Brigid's relationship to it raises the question as to whether women were occasionally worked the forge as well. I am living proof that a woman can swing a hammer at an anvil as I have done it. In many myths, Brigid is credited with bringing smithwork to the world, but she was not the only smith in the vast Celtic pantheon. The Irish God Gobniu is often called "The Smith." The theory that argues Brigid originated solely as Brigantia and came to Ireland with the refugee British Druids also often argues that the Irish Druids, looking for space for the new Goddess in their pantheon, moved existing smith deities aside. Yet, as Brigid was equally as likely to have already been in Ireland, she very well might have had jurisdiction over the smithy all. The greatest truth again comes back to the idea of exalted, and the idea of a feminine spirit embodying sacred elements. *Brig*, the Lady of the

Smith and Forge, breathed life into this most important technology and, through its spirit, the people thrived.

If the importance of smithing to the Celts is any clue, Brigid the Smith might better be termed the Goddess of Work That Changes the Course of Human Evolution. Brigid-Smithworker radically changes the paradigm. The hammer on the anvil is more than a symbol—it is an action of revolutionizing the status quo. Calling upon the Fiery Aspect of Brigid will purge, shape, and purify, and will leave all that it touches radically changed for the better.

THE STRETCH ON THE ANVIL

The work of the blacksmith is all about control, compression, and stretching. It requires extreme amounts of heat, sweat, and concentrated effort. The smith prepares the raw ore first by exposing it to a brilliantly hot forge. The extreme temperatures soften the metal. When it reaches the proper softness, the metal is moved to the anvil where it is pounded and shaped as desired, starting the interaction between form and function, achieving the strength and shape that the smith desires. The smith watches the metal carefully so that it softens but never melts, and therefore never destroyed. This process removes the impurities of the metal that previously weakened it, leaving the finished product strong, durable, and capable of the work for which it was designed. The heat and the hammer flake away weaker pieces of the metal. After a number of rounds of heating and pounding, the smith will eventually give the metal a cooling plunge into the water, but never before the work is complete. It is probably not a huge surprise that this work is in line with what Brigid's work will do for practitioners. Brigid the Smith could be called "Brigid the Soul-Pounder."

My coven calls this debacle of tears, rage, routine hair-pulling, eventual calm, and inevitable strength, The Stretch on the Anvil. It is a time of testing, pressure, and compression in the way that the smith shapes metal. Throughout our lives, we pick up bad habits. We cling to painful relationships. We mold ourselves into unnatural shapes. In a sense, we create our own toxic prisons that we come to believe shelter us or strengthen us. The trials of Brigid's Anvil include the crumbling of the walls we worked desperately to build, relationships we wept to keep, poor health habits we defended, even obligations we insisted on keeping. Like the impurities shed under the smith's hammer, Brigid pounds our own impurities away. It is not an easy process. It's easy to want to cling to that which is comforting, no matter if it's something unhealthy or unnatural. One of the rules about magick, one of my teachers often says, is that the first thing it changes is the Self. Brigid's transformative magick work comes in the barely disguised form of a symbolic anvil and hammer.

After the metal has been heated and shaped, its process work is far from over. The metal cools, cracks, and settles. Its color settles on the surface, but its internal system takes longer. After Brigid's anvil, our external lives may be radically different, but our hearts and souls take longer to settle. It opens a whole new level of fears, insecurities, and other unnecessaries that again need to be pulled out, re-forged, re-hammered, and re-cooled. In the end of the smith's process, the coal burns out and the specks of metal melted from the ore fall to the bottom of the forge, where it becomes a waste product called *clinker*. It's useless to the smith, and in some ways it mirrors what we discard in the process of Brigid's Anvil. Yet, when I was in the blacksmith shop and looking at the strange pieces of clinker, previously black coal, burned white and looking like a mutilated piece of salt, a passerby mentioned that clinker was a component of new, budding planets. After stars explode, they release a clinker-like product through space, which eventually comes together with other clinker pieces to create a new space body. I do not know how much truth there is to that and how much interplanetary geology I'm missing. In a spiritual sense, however, maybe it's possible that what we throw away in our own anvil process has room for growth and expansion somewhere else, in a new form.

One can imagine an anvil, look at pictures, or browse the Internet for videos and articles. One can also visualize, visualize, visualize until the center of the mind melts. But one cannot know what an anvil is about until one has been to it, smelled the coal and the hot metal, touched it, and heard the ring of the hammer strike from down the road. There are times when the hammer to metal seems so natural the hammer itself seem an extension of your arm, but it can spark and sting, which reminds you to be diligent and vigilant. This is true of the spiritual anvil as well. The whole intention of the smith is to create strength in the material he or she works with. The ability to wield metal thicker and stronger was the essential hallmark of the master smith. This is also the role of Brigid the Smith. The pain and the stress that may come when invoking Brigid the Smith is invariably, intentionally part of the process of strengthening the soul. Some people may never experience the anvil. They may not need it. Some may enjoy the process. Others may descend through the fires to even deeper mysteries. If you find yourself on a pressured, chaotic journey while working with Brigid, take heart. She is working to make you stronger.

Reflection: What has made you stronger or wiser? Where have you been stretched and pounded? Where have you grown and what parts of you do you consider iron-fortified? Durable? Usable as a result of your trials? Consider also what parts of you were chipped away by your own anvil moments? Did they take a new life else-where, in the way a smithy's clinker might?

BRIGID HAD HER OWN ANVIL

In the following myth, it is Gobniu who holds the role of the Smithgod, but the work of the smithy and Brigid's own subsequent anvil moment explores the power of flame and fire to permanently change.

Nuada, the King with the Silver Hand, could not sit on the throne of the Tuatha de Danann because he was missing a hand, one replaced with silver. This meant he was blemished, and according to Tuatha de Danann law, was unfit to rule his people. No other potential King was present and so to fill the role and unify the People of the Sky with the People of the Ocean, the Tuatha de Danann summoned Bres of the Sea People, the Fomorians, to be their leader. As a chosen King, his leadership unified a bond between the former enemies. To seal the arrangement and strengthen the union, Brigid agreed to marry Bres. Together, they had three sons.

Bres began his reign as a good leader and all the People of the Sea and the Sky were happy. But slowly at first and then greatly, Bres taxed the children of Dana. He claimed all milk from all cattle, all grain from each field, all sparks from each fire. Gods of old renown were forced to labor in the fields until they dropped from exhaustion. None could fulfill their duties and the people starved.

Brigid kept her silence lest to tempt her husband's anger and incite more disaster for her people. When Bres became bored and greedy and began thinking of new ways to extort Dana's children further, Brigid would brew beer, sing songs, and share tales, until her husband fell into a deep sleep. While he napped, Brigid gathered cheese and bread into her green cloak and shared the food with her starving people.

In time, fortified by the strength Brigid provided, the Tuatha de Danann planned an attack. They cast a spell and chanted the words "Sinew to sinew . . . and nerve to nerve . . ." and repaired Nuada's hand, the new flesh restored. Led by their rightful King, Bres was overthrown and sent back to the ocean, taking the sons he had by Brigid with him. Brigid paced along the shore, as she could not go with her sons and their father to the depths of the sea, but stayed at the place where the shore and sea met, lest either her children or her people need her.

The Tuatha de Danann grew strong, and with their strength, Bres's anger grew, too. He, along with his Fomorian people, returned from the sea to fight the Tuatha to reclaim the throne. But the Tuatha de Danann soldiers had magickal weapons. No matter how their swords and spears splintered, they were made anew at dawn the next day. Irate, Bres called forth Ruadan, the eldest son he shared with Brigid, to seek the secrets of the Tuatha's magickal, renewing metal. Dressed as a Tuatha warrior, Ruadan came out of the sea and met Gobniu, the Smith, working alongside Luchtainé, the carpenter, and Credné the bronze worker. He watched how the three worked together before returning to his father's people.

Ruadan shared the stories of the weaponry metal fixed so adroitly that they never needed re-hammering or repair and of the cooperation of the men, their skill, and their generosity. Bres sent him back to the Tuatha, this time to kill Gobniu. Ruadan approached the Smith again and asked for a javelin, which Gobniu gave without question. Ruadan thrust the spear through Gobniu's breast, a blow that would have killed the strongest of men and Gods . . . yet the old Smith plucked the weapon from his breast like the tiniest of splinters and hurled it back at his assailant. Ruadan was mortally wounded and he limped back to the sea to die.

As their son lay on the shoreline, his life leaving this world, Brigid and Bres mourned together—the sound of their cries piercing the stormy air across the land. Their weeping would henceforth be known as keening and it is this act of great mourning that is known as an invention of Brigid's, from the time she lost her son to treachery and greed.

—Interpreted from traditional tale

For all of her spunk and joviality, Brigid was no stranger to pain or sorrow or straddling stressful situations to make peace. I must admit, I took quite a bit of poetic license with the story above. The myths I found have Brigid and Bres marry, but then Brigid disappears from the story until Ruadan's death, when she invents keening in her grief. It seems odd and unlikely that such a resourceful Goddess would stand back idly while her husband created massive chaos and her people suffered. Yet, she was in a tough position. Perhaps she loved Bres. Perhaps she only stayed with him for political reasons, or to protect her children. In this story, Brigid embodies the all-too-human experience of watching loved ones make terrible mistakes, of needing to walk a fine line between argumentative parties, and of making selfless sacrifices for the betterment of others. Ultimately, Brigid embodies the element of pain so great it cannot be spoken, only screamed.

As with Anvil and Forge, Brigid again invented a mechanism for coping with suffering—keening. Keening was a nearly lyrical type of wailing performed in honor of the dead. It has been described as a deeply personal cathartic expression in which the wailing would move to others in the space, until all present would wail to a point of frenzy. The practice was outlawed by the

Catholic Church in the mid-1800s. Some say the Pagan nature of keening triggered the Church's distaste. For well over a century, keening was pretty much obsolete and relegated to folklore and works of fiction. Because of its intimate nature and dissolution before recording equipment was easily accessible, examples of old-world keening are tough to find, if they can be found at all. Yet the practice may be returning. Keeners appear at funeral or ancestral rites, but also at political demonstrations.

It's a stretch to call grief a gift, but there is a gift in a method of coping with sorrow. Giving voice to our sadness and pain, be it through a chorus of wails or another cathartic method such as words on a page, is a type of Brigid work.

Reflection: The following poem was written in response to the elementary school shooting at Newtown, Connecticut in 2012.

Prayer for the Grieving

Dear Mother Goddess Brigit
whose own son turned
in murderous treachery
against his mother's people
and died

You know the grieving of our hearts

Bless us Brigit
in our anger and our shock
in our broken hearted sorrow
Bring healing to those who live
and peace to those who died

Build us whole again
Sing our rebirth

that we may live

in awareness and compassion

on this beautiful

troubled Earth

—MAEL BRIGDE

RITUAL: BRIGID'S ETERNAL FIRE AND THE SOUL'S SURRENDER: THE RITE OF THE NINETEENTH NIGHT

Fire in the physical world is of principal importance. We must have fire, but fire can injure and destroy as well. The symbolic idea of fire is associated with creation, drive, and passion, but the strenuous parts of fire can be forgotten or glossed over. Like the fires of the forge, the light in the temple, or our internal flames of desire, spiritual fire must be tended. Sometimes, though, we run out of fuel. Spiritual flames remind us that we rely on cooperation with others. Keeping the flame lit at the shrine of Kildare required cooperation on behalf of Brigid's Priestesses and later, her nuns. Yet on the nineteenth night, the tender of the flame would surrender the work to Brigid as the part of the community had been exhausted. Brigid was expected to step in and complete the work on the twentieth night. When we reach points of trouble and complications in our journeys, and we have finally exhausted all that we are able to do, this is the point at which we call on the help of the Divine. We can keep pushing, or we can surrender our trying and striving and ask Brigid to tend our flames.

When you've reached a point in a tasking part of your journey in which you can do nothing more to improve a situation either internally or outside of you, and you wish for Brigid's help for the rest, the following is a suggested ritual for doing this work.

Materials

20 votive or tea light candles

A fresh apple, cored

An image or written description of the trouble you wish to surrender

Start this ritual when you have sufficient time and quiet. Light nineteen candles in a circle. Leave one candle unlit in the center of the circle, with the apple next to it. As the nineteen candles burn, reflect on your period of difficulty. Think of what you've tried to do to fix the situation, acknowledging mistakes made along the way and also the things that are outside of your control.

While in this space, you may find inspiration for new approaches to your task. Then again, you may not. The objective here is to surrender.

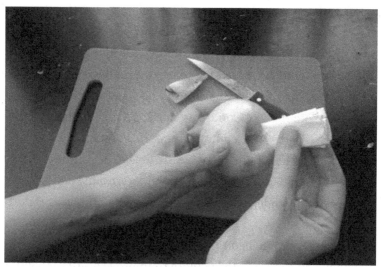

You will actually write on and place the paper in the apple during your ritual, but this image demonstrates how to do so when the time comes.

When you are ready to surrender your trouble, write it down on the piece of paper. If you were able to print a photo of said trouble, write "I surrender this" on the picture. Roll up the message or picture into a scroll and insert it into the cored apple.

Extinguish all flames, but light the one in the center. Say aloud:

Brigid, Mother of Flame, Fire, and Forge,
In the heat and the darkness,
I seek patience in the tightness,
I seek peace within the kiln,
I seek compassion in the strife,
Create in me the quiet well of night,
As I surrender my tasks to you.
Brigid, the nineteen nights have been tended.
Brigid, now be the twentieth night of my soul's journey.
Brigid, tend your flame.

You may want to speak other petitions for help at this point. Stay with the candle while it burns out.

When the rite ends or on the following day, bury the apple or toss it into a river or stream with the paper inside of it.

EXERCISE: A PRACTICE FOR EMPOWERMENT WITH BRIGID'S FIRE

This simple but highly effective practice with Brigid's flame is designed to reenergize when personal resources are low, or to simply better connect you with Brigid's flame.

Materials

Five small white candles. Tea lights or votives are fine. (I like to use Sabbath candles.)

Brigid's oil (as found in Chapter 10).

Anoint each candle and wick with the Brigid oil. Set the candles in secure holders or on flame-resistant dishes. Light and arrange them so that, while you are lying on the floor, there is one candle just above your head, one to your right hand, one to your left, and one at each of your feet.

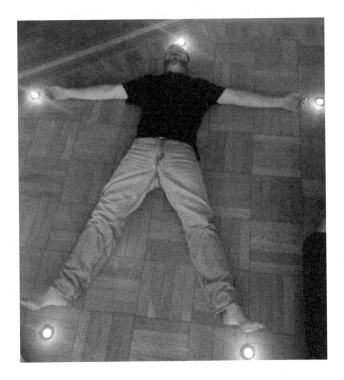

While in this position, envision each of these candles emanating a powerful white light that does not consume, but connects to each part of you from where you lie and fuses with your physical structure. See this white light travel through your limbs and head, and how each beam of light connects at your heart. Begin to see the white light pulse with each of your heart's beats.

Envision your heartbeat is the clink of the hammer on the anvil. With each pound, envision that the eternal flame, symbolized by the five candles, is traveling into your body and linking with your heart. Stay in this position until the light seems to create glowing bars of iron from each flame, glowing brightly to where they meet at your heart.

This is not the space to overthink. Some fall into a deep sleep. Give yourself plenty of time in this position. When you feel ready to, conclude the rite, and extinguish the candles.

CHAPTER 6

Goddess of the Oak: The Sacrificial Brigid

In that place there stood a mighty oak tree, much beloved by Brigid, indeed blessed by her. The trunk survives to this day and none dare cut it with an axe. It possesses a property so great that any person able to break off a part of it with their hands can hope thereby to win God's aid. Many miracles, by the blessings of Blessed Brigid, have been received through that oak tree.

—ANIMOSUS, c. 980 C.E. Description of an oak tree, presumably the one at the Shrine at Kildare, dead at the time of Animosus's writing.

O ne fog-drenched night on my first visit to Ireland, I stood on the back patio of a rented cottage with two friends. As each mist-billow passed, the line of trees at the edge of the property seemed to move closer to us. We stood frozen, admitting we were seeing the same thing. Could trees really walk like they did in the stories we heard as children and was it really happening in front of us? We finally ran back into the cottage when it looked as though the trees had advanced to the line where the patio met the grass. In the morning light, the trees were back on the other side of the lawn. We were confused, scared, and completely thrilled.

Something magickal had happened. It hadn't been substance; we had all been quite sober. Maybe it was an optical illusion created by the fog, or a touch of lingering jet lag. Or maybe Ireland is just magickal enough a place that trees walk across lawns in the middle of the night. I still have the muscle memory of petrified terror and delight, and probably always will.

From the base of Gog, the more than 2,000-year-old oak tree in Glastonbury.

There is something profound to ancient trees and their presence in Celtic culture of old. When I visited Glastonbury for this book's research, I also visited the famous ancient oaks, Gog and Magog, each over 2,000 years old. One is now dead but its trunk still stands. The other is still alive. These oaks are believed to have been part of an entryway to the Tor, perhaps part of a long ceremonial walk, used by the Druids. I wept when I first touched the great trunk of one of the oaks. I can be stoic and analytical about these kinds of things. My profound moments trickle in over periods of time and reflection, but this one smacked like a wave. I've never had such an immediate and visceral reaction to any object without any context at all before or since. Something about oak is profoundly significant. Oak may be a lesser-known area of patronage for Brigid, but it is perhaps what most reveals her Druidic legacy.

CELTIC AND DRUIDIC LEGACY OF OAK

With sacred mistletoe the Druids crown'd
Sung with the nymphs, and danc'd the pleasing round.
— WILLIAM DIAPER

In the ancient Celtic world, the land was covered with thick forests and the oak trees were massive. The oak was considered the Druid's tree. Some have even argued that the very word "Druid" is derived from an old term for oak. Having yet to be cleared, the oaks had grown to proportions dwarfing most of the oaks alive today. Its size, antiquity, and remarkable resistance to fire, disease, and insects may have inspired the Druidic title for the oak as the *King of the Trees* or *The Magickal Tree*. For reasons unknown to me, the oak is more likely than other trees to be struck by lightning. Because of this, the Druids may have connected the oak to thunder and sky Gods. Oak acorns found on the forest floor fattened domestic pigs, ensuring healthy livestock, and oak bark could tan leather. The sturdy, water-resistant wood of the oak provided construction of sea-worthy ships for trade and travel. Naturally, the oak was greatly revered by the Celts and, in particular, the Druids themselves.

Whether for their power and strength, the seemingly indestructible quality of the rootless mistletoe growing out of oak bark, or the food supply for their livestock, the oak had a profound significance in Celtic spirituality. Oak received special veneration from Druids, who had fixed dates and prescribed ceremonies for cutting the sacred mistletoe with a golden hatchet. Both oak and mistletoe were primary focuses of Druidic worship. The boughs of the great trees provided the temples for their rites. Some earlier writers suggested that religious rites occurred in urban areas while some writers, particularly those who wrote of the mythical shrines on Anglesey Island in Wales, claimed the Druidic rites only ever happened in dark, thick forest and sacred groves. This might indicate that the increased Roman influence pushed the Druid and the Celtic religious practices farther into remote areas, or it may simply indicate different sects of Druids practicing in different areas.

Regional oaks marked the center of community worship and were pillars of honor and local cultural identity. Some myths indicate the felling of an oak was a political blow, such as one myth in which the King of Tara Hill cut down a massive oak in another region to humiliate that region's ruler. The mighty oak was also an obstacle for the ancient Celts. Because of its size, it was probably a very difficult tree to clear, which limited the spread of agriculture. The oak was known as a barrier between the realm of the humans and that of the land spirits and Gods.

Natural oak groves were honored as a sanctuary for the local land spirits. Trees growing by sources of water, such as over a wells were of particular importance and considered portals to the Spirit world. Shrines were likely built near such places. Later, when these very shrines were converted to Christian churches and magick wells to holy wells, often the oaks were left in peace rather than cut. Time eventually felled the oldest of the oaken groves and few remain. But even the early Celtic Christians recognized the prominence of the oak as a spiritual entity and enveloped it into the new religion.

It is also not insignificant that the Dagda, "the Good God," sometimes carried the title of *Daire*, a name meaning "oak" as well as "fruitful one." The Dagda had an oak harp that would never play without him being present. To get it to play, he would say to the instrument:

Come, oak of two cries!
Come, hand of fourfold music!
Come, summer! Come, winter!
Voice of harps, bellows, and flutes!

The two names for the harp, "Oak of Two Cries" may have meant the oak in flower and the oak in wither. "Hand of Fourfold Music" may have referred to the oak's presence at the four fire festivals marking the four Celtic seasons. The Dagda as the earthen provider held a link to the regeneration of the earth and its bounty through this oaken instrument. In the hands of the Dagda, the oak was a consistent symbol of life. In a myth of the hero Cuchulainn, the antagonists known as the children of Cailitin attack Cuchulainn's fortress with dead oak leaves—not a terribly vile weapon in its own right, but the symbolism of the dead oak leaves evokes images of death and decomposing. A live oak was a blessing. Dead oak may have meant a curse.

In a Welsh myth, the God Gwydion, helped by his brother Amaethon, the God of agriculture, and his son Lleu fought the "Battle of Trees": a war meant to secure three bounties for man: the dog, the deer, and the lapwing. It was a battle of man against advancing trees. The smallest trees were the easiest to "conquer," but the oak stood in defense of all of the others. This battle serves as an illustration of humanity's encroachment on the forest, "taming it" for agriculture and settlement building. Yet, the oak was the most difficult to tame. It was the great gate-keeper between the world of men and the world of Gods. The tools of the time were no match for a giant oak's strength and girth. In today's increasingly environmentally sensitive world, it may be hard to celebrate a battle against trees or nature. Yet, at the time these myths and poems took form, nature was still very much a force to fight and tame as humans were still quite vulnerable to it. Oak meant life. Oak meant challenge. Oak was both the provider of health for communities, and also drew a strong line where humanity's realm ended and that of the land spirits began. In that sense, the oak was the land's image of the great land Goddess. For its mighty position, the oak demanded the greatest respect of the Celts and as we will also see, the greatest sacrifice.

OAK: TREE OF SACRIFICE

The presence of oak in Brigid lore seems inexplicable if the Druidic history is not considered. The world of the ancient Celts was fraught with terrifying things. Appeasing the Gods required immense sacrifice. When a new settlement was founded, a domesticated animal (often a bull or a horse) was often sacrificed and buried in the center of the dwelling to appease the local Spirits, invoking their favor on the burgeoning community. Some animal sacrifice occurred at socio-political-religious festivals, where the animals were consumed as part of a ritual feast. But in some instances . . ., animal sacrifice wasn't considered enough to appease the Gods. The best of the sacrificial offerings was man, and bloody rites in the name of pleasing the Gods were performed in the oak groves of the Druids.

One account of a Druidic oak grove was anything but the romantic or peaceful images commonly seen in paintings or literature. "No birds or beasts dared enter it, and not even the wind, but the branches moved of their own accord and water fell from dark springs." The frightened writer then described the groves as dark and gloomy, oak branches woven tightly together to block out the sun, and in the center, a series of altars heaped with human remains, with blood deliberately splattered on the surrounding oak trunks. Horrifying heads were carved into the oak stumps to ward off the uninvited. Trees could fall and rise again, phantom flames would appear among the trunks, and serpents glided between them. No humans planning to leave the grove ever entered it, aside from its Priests.

Other stories include the sacrificial victims being nailed to the oaks, the Druids then divining events of the future through the death throes, positions of entrails, and where the blood landed on the grove trunks. These victims might have been shot with arrows or impaled in the shrines and then suspended on the trees, their final movements deciphered as oracles. Some victims were burned alive with oak timber as fuel, as in the legendary Wicker Man. The Gods could not be fully appeased until human life was offered and some have said that the deaths meant the bounty of the harvest. Whatever the method, oak had a role in these rites. Some scribes wrote that the Druids refused to perform their rites if, at the very least, oak leaves were not present. Others wrote that oak wood was the primary fuel for flames in the Druidic shrines.

These stories of sacrifice are undoubtedly nasty, but before anyone runs away screaming, it is important to keep in mind that the Romans had plenty of need for propaganda against the Celts. Roman people historically did not support the destruction of religions shrines, perhaps out of fear of the foreign Gods' retribution, but likely also out of respect for the shrines, themselves. Politically, it was in Rome's best interests to annihilate the Druidic caste, which would dismantle the core of the Celtic world and therefore make the lands easier to conquer. Portraying Druidic shrines as horrific places of human slaughter would rally support—and possibly more willing tax money—for shrine—and therefore, Druidic—destruction. It may also have been fear. Victims were frequently captured soldiers or community criminals, although they routinely included persons of prestige, willingly giving their lives over to the Gods for the benefit of their communities. It is highly likely that details are exaggerated. Yet human sacrifice was a regularity in religion in most parts of the world at that time in human history. Romans did quite a bit of it themselves. Some Roman writers reported that the Celts only practiced human sacrifice during times of extreme danger or perceived emergency. Toward the end of the sovereign Celtic era, circumstances across the land may have been so stressed and chaos-laced as the Roman occupation increased that it might have inspired more actions as such. While the lurid nature of the tales is possibly overblown, the reality of human sacrifice in the ancient Celtic world was not—nor is the connection between these practices and the oak. The Lindow Man, a sacrificial victim who was preserved in the bogs of England for nearly two thousand years, is one of the more famous archeological discoveries. He was found with traces of mistletoe resin in the stomach of his ancient corpse, confirming the suspicion that the great oaks were connected with great sacrifice.

So, why oak? Why did these trees bear the brunt of Druidic sacrifice? The oak was an embodiment of the spirit of the land—a living face of the Goddess herself. Performing the rites on oak or with oak lumber provided the most direct link for the Druids to make their sacrifices for the land Deities. The Celts may have also recognized the sacrifice the land made naturally for the betterment of the living via the dropping of the oaks' leaves and acorns. Perhaps in the expansion of agriculture and reaping of iron ore, the Celts were aware of their impact on the environment and believed that only a sacrifice of a human could compare to the sacrifice the earth made. A cryptic phrase derived from these rites describes, "Eyes to the sun, breath to the wind, life force to the atmosphere, ear to the cardinal points, flesh to the earth," which may speak of dismantling the human body to return it to the Divine source, possibly in a manner consistent with how the Celts saw the land being dismantled for their own use. To use the King of the Trees both as fuel for the rites and as subject of placation showed the Celts' deference to the Gods as well as their determination to surmount any obstacle the Gods could throw. The seemingly immortal nature of the oak may have also played a part. Perhaps the Celts wished to garner some of the ageless quality of the tree for their own people. The questions are complex and deserve their own book. If it suffices to say that oak remained a paramount fixture in the Celtic spiritual lore and its connection to sacrifice an indelible one, its image allows us to understand more about Brigid's relationship to sacrifice as well.

BRIGID AND THE OAK

Brigid's myths speak heavily and frequently of her powers over fire and water and completion of important tasks, but oak isn't readily found. In fact, the only tree mentioned in Brigid myths is apple, not oak:

> *Once a woman had a bounty of apples in her orchard. Not a branch could be found that wasn't bowed with the weight of the plump fruit. A woman gave Brigid a blooming basket of apples, seeking her blessing and praise. Soon after, a pair of hungry and downcast people came to Brigid to ask for food. She immediately gave them the basket of apples, along with a blessing and praise, and sent them on their way. The woman was angry. "I brought these apples for you! Not for those people. Why did you give away my gift?" Brigid smiled and bid the woman goodbye and quietly cursed the tree from which the apples had come. Still angry, the woman walked home to discover an empty orchard. All the apples had fallen from the trees and lay rotten on the ground. The orchard never bloomed again as Brigid saw to its barrenness.*
>
> —TRADITIONAL TALE

Despite its absence from her myths, oak surrounds Brigid's image in churches, statues, and in stained glass portraits. Even the name *Kildare* where Brigid's famed shrine continues to be kept, comes from the name *Cill-Dara*, literally meaning "Church of the Oak." At this shrine, the ancient oak mentioned at the start of the chapter survived until nearly the tenth century, when it likely died of natural causes. Like the Glastonbury oaks, it could have easily been a thousand years old, or older. For centuries after the shrine's conversion to a church, the oak stood and its reverence continued in Celtic Christianity. The shrine's perpetual fire is believed to have been fed oak timber as fuel. When Bishop Delany restored the Brigidine order in the nineteenth century (after its Reformation suppression) to help continuity of the Brigidine order, he brought an oak sapling from Kildare to plant at a new Brigidine convent in County Carlow.

Over the centuries, Brigid has not strayed from her connection to the oak tree. Many of the older churches named for St. Brigid had roofs, slats, and pews made from oak. In some of the Norman-era St. Brigid churches the clergy's vestments are detailed with oak leaves, such as the famous Skenfrith Cope, which is also stored in an oak case. Some of these garments are centuries old. Also at the St. Bridget church at Skenfrith, an image of Brigid hewn completely out of solid oak greets parishioners from the pulpit. In Voudon, some stories suggest that Maman Brigitte lives in an oak tree in the cemetery. Over the last few decades, oak saplings have been planted at St. Brigid's church in Kildare, encouraging the tree to reclaim its rightful place.

Images of St. Brigid, hewn completely out of oak, on the pulpit of the St. Bridget Church in Skenfrith, Monmouthshire.

While the apple tree story does not indicate Brigid's patronage over oak, it does indicate her abilities as a land Goddess. The Goddess of Land can and will give, but will also take away at random. The tree connection reveals her as a fierce protector of the poor, much in the way that the oak was known for being the defender of the smaller, weaker trees as in the mythic battle. The story also illustrates the nature of true sacrifice—giving for the betterment of others, not of the self. The oak's roots are deep and run wide, dropping enough acorns to create a family of trees. If the oak tree was a symbol of the living embodiment of the land, it is natural that it would be connected to a Deity such as Brigid whose living embodiment *was* the land—including the topography and foliage. It is through her embodiment as the land Goddess that Brigid is connected to oak and it is through oak that she embodies the Sacrificial Goddess.

Reflection: What is the nature of giving unconditionally? Why do we give? Is response in kind expected? Is sacrifice a willing exchange or an assumed one? For what would we be willing to sacrifice and what do we expect in return? Can we even expect a result of sacrifice?

BRIGID: THE SACRIFICIAL GODDESS

When Brigid was young, her beauty was renowned. But she had promised chastity to the Christian God, who would lay a curse upon any man who tempted her to break her vow. One day a young man caught sight of her walking alongside the road and began to follow her. Fearful for the man's life should he be the cause of Brigid's broken chastity, she hurried away. The man turned and mounted a horse, pursuing her relentlessly through the hills and valleys. Brigid ran faster and ducked beneath a bridge, kneeling by a stream. She plucked out her eyes out to avoid being recognized. The man, horrified by the sight, turned on his horse and fled. Brigid then healed herself in the stream, her eyes renewed, and she continued about her journey.

—TRADITIONAL TALE

This story is an easy sore on contemporary readers. We so often are exposed to horrifying stories of women being punished for the "crime" of being raped or abused by assailants, the idea of a woman literally plucking her own eyes out for the sake of a potential assailant's soul may feel like a thorn in that rightfully painful place. But if we look at this through the lens of Brigid as the Earth Goddess, Brigid is making a sacrifice to ensure the well-being of the earth's inhabitants, like the harvest Goddess Tailtu, who died clearing the forest for the fields to be planted, or Boann, who gave her body to be the river. As the eyes of Celtic sacrificial victims were offered up to the sun, Brigid's plucking them out could be protecting the man from dangers he does not recognize himself, perhaps reminiscent of a sacrifice to the Sun Gods believed to protect the community from the dangers that come from long winters. In the end, like the Earth Goddess she is, Brigid regenerates herself.

Reflection: When have you had to make a sacrifice that others did not understand? Have you had to sacrifice for others, without their even knowing about it or that there was a need to do so in the first place? To what depths would you go to give of yourself, completely, without credit or acknowledgement?

Was Brigid ever the desired recipient of the bloody sacrificial gifts? Or did worship of Brig the Exalted One not require such appeasement? In truth, we'll never know, but in probability, sacrifice happened for Brigid. Even the most comely practices surrounding Brigid, be she saint or Goddess, carry definitive links to a time when the greatest gift to give was that of the human life. Some older rites include the offering of chicken blood at a crossroads at Imbolc. The pattern of the blood on the ground would indicate whether Brigid was displeased, a connection to the rumored practice of Druids watching for signs in the death throes of their victims.

A series of rites known as the Threshold Rites took place for centuries in rural Ireland, honoring Brigid as sacrificial Earth Mother in a subtle way. More comprehensive information can be found in *The Rites of Brigid, Goddess and Saint* by Seán ó Duinn. In the Threshold Rites, rushes were gathered and bundled on the eve of Imbolc (January 31). Sometimes, the rushes were formally shaped into a human form and wrapped in cloth to look like a dress. If one member of the house had a particularly dangerous line of work, such as fishing, their clothing was often used to dress the doll, further aiding in their protection. The rush bundles were left on the doorstep before the sun set while a supper was prepared inside. When supper was ready, someone (usually the "man of the house") would go to the step, close the door, and take the bundle of rushes in his arms while reciting something called a *threshold dialogue* with everyone inside, announcing Brigid's arrival and requesting that she come in. Sometimes, the bundle was carried around the house three times until someone inside called out *Cead Failte Romhat, a Bhrid!* (roughly, "Brigid Is Very Welcome!").

Finally, the "woman of the house," wearing a veil of some sort, opened the door and Brigid, symbolized by the bundle of rushes, was welcomed into the home. The rush bundle was set near the stove and if the dinner were being cooked in a large pot, the pot would be set on top of the bundle. The family then served themselves from the pot. After the supper, the pot was removed and the rushes divided among the family, each person forming them into a St. Brigid's cross. The crosses were often nailed to the beams inside the home for protection. The breaking of Brigid's rush-body, the ritual feast, and the weaving of the dismembered doll into protective amulets was a gentle descendant of the earlier rites, when a human would be the sacrifice. In the Threshold Rite, Brigid was honored as Earth Mother and her sacrifice was recognized and celebrated, and energies of peace and protection invoked against dangers present outside of the home.

Through its recurring image in Brigid iconography and their mutual myth and history connected with sacrifice and protection, oak quietly symbolizes Brigid's identity as the Earth Goddess who gives so that living creatures may flourish. The oak can also be seen as a symbol of Brigid's endurance through time. It is a plant of immense longevity, nearly bordering on immortality. The curious mistletoe is its own testament to Brigid's enduring presence—blossoming after leaving its base, and as Irish descendants took her image around the world. Like mistletoe, she blooms without root.

MESSAGE FROM OAK

The oak is an inspiration. Its stillness and strength continue to mystify humans in a largely de-mystified world. At the 9/11 Memorial in New York City, architects planted white oak saplings so that in a number of years, these beautiful trees will shade the area. Oak's ancestry of slow growth yet inevitable strength, and symbolic ability to stand through time is not lost on the contemporary. The reality that a small, fragile nut can find its way to root in any place (I've seen oak grow from bricks and concrete!) can almost seem fantasy. Oak's slow growth shares a commonality with Brigid. An oak grows slowly and takes decades to mature, much like the development of the Bard or the Smith. The oak must sacrifice its leaves and acorns and eventually its own self, its trunk becoming the food and fodder for other plants just as the Bard sacrifices years of their life to their training in hopes that their work will be a platform for subsequent Bards to learn their craft. The time, patience, and endurance of both the oak and the Bard weave into Brigid's ever-expanding cloak of influence. When passing by an oak, stop to say hello as you're also sending good wishes to Brigid as well.

EXERCISE: SACRIFICE IN THE OAK RITE

Using oak in your Brigid Magick is a powerful way to connect with her as Earth Mother. It also calls to mind the connection to personal sacrifice. Brigid of Oak asks us to consider what we deem important—for ourselves, for our families, and for our communities. The kind of sacrifice Brigid as Oak and Earth Mother makes should not be confused with martyrdom. The earth gives only what is in its power and resources to give and all earthen resources are finite. When the earth is pushed beyond its capacity to give, it stops or even retaliates. For one example, if a forest is fully felled and cleared, some of the results include landslides that can wipe away hillside homes or other natural areas. Carbon harvested from the earth and burned continues to heat up the atmosphere, and the earth responds by increasing the number of violent storms, which may be a self-regulatory cooling method. The ancient Celts had individuals, willing or not, give the greatest sacrifice of their lives, but we also must keep in mind that such extremes weren't necessary for most people. There may come a time when an individual must sacrifice something that hurts to give, but the risk of not giving is even greater, such as a parent selling a home to pay for their child's surgery. Most sacrifice might mean picking up an extra work shift or working a slightly longer day a couple of times a week, a sacrifice of some leisure time in order to enrich a home's prosperity. Sacrifice doesn't automatically mean taking a full-on second job and sacrificing all sleep, unless the situation was dire enough to call for it. Among my clients, students, fellow members of the community, and even myself, big sacrifices are given all too easily and quickly for things that are insignificant in the long run, but we are reticent to sacrifice for things that matter to us greatly. I am equally guilty of this, and I have no idea why any of us do such nonsense. We might be willing to sacrifice sanity and time and emotional energy on reflecting, ruminating, and verbally disseminating the actions of a rude co-worker or former flame, yet be unwilling to sacrifice time or other resources to help a community cause, even if the sight of a shoeless person in winter hurts our hearts. Regular acts of small sacrifice strengthen the Spirit. They teach us where our boundaries and abilities to give are. Before communing with Brigid's Oak energy, participate in a small act of sacrifice to enter into that energetic understanding.

If you live in an area where oak grows, collecting acorns for your altar or magick space is helpful in connecting you with this side of Brigid. If you happen to live or work with people who are energetically or emotionally draining, carrying three acorns will help fortify you against these influences. (Note: If you are in a situation where you are being outright abused, do not rely on acorns—seek help.) If you are in a position in which you have to sacrifice something important to you, such as a home as in the example above, having acorns present with you will lend strength to your sacrifice and also serve as a reminder that, like the oak who sacrifices acorns that ultimately will lead to a rebirth, so can our initial sacrifice lead to new things.

When you collect the acorns, make sacrifice in honor of the oak when you do it. Many magick practitioners leave hair, saliva, or even blood, or a food or drink offering. Food scraps will ultimately compost and make for new soil, if they're not toxic to local animals. An excellent and simple sacrifice a human can make in honor of oak, or any tree, is collecting trash or volunteering with a parks or forestry department. When writing this chapter, my partner and I spent an afternoon collecting garbage in a park near our apartment. It was indeed a sacrifice of time and stomach stability as the stench of NYC park trash is rarely paralleled by anything, anywhere. After we finished our work, I spent some time with a beautiful young oak slightly off the park's beaten path. I wanted to take some of the acorns strewn on the ground home to my Brigid altar and, while touching the tree's truck, opened my senses to feel if this would be all right. In my head, I heard a resounding, "NO." I had an image of a mother being separated from her baby and felt a grip of panic. It seemed odd. There were so many acorns lying around that it couldn't hurt the whole forest if I took a couple home. Why did I get such a sensation? I heeded the feeling, however, and did not take the acorns. Later, on doing some more research, I learned that the time of year we'd picked to do this work was when the acorns were more likely to take root than any other time of the year. It made sense as to why the tree did not want the acorns removed.

It may sound bizarre that a tree could share such a message, but keep in mind that a tree is a living thing—most trees are much older than you or I—and a tree has electrical impulses of its own and responds to injury (think of sap rising when a hole in a tree is tapped). It is probably very aware in its own way when a part of itself is in danger. Maybe it was my own head doing the tree-talking and an ancestral part of me knew this was a bad time to take the acorns, or maybe evolution has provided the oak with a vibe of "Get away from my acorns . . . I must regenerate" during the season of the year when regeneration is most likely to happen. It is important to be mindful when performing your sacrifice that you don't assume that the tree owes you its seed. Humans have already taken away a great deal from trees and forests and we're not owed much more. It's not a case for anxiety, but a suggestion to stop, feel, and trust your instincts. Your own instincts may tell you the collection of wood or acorns is perfectly justified, and in that case, you are probably right. If you don't live in an area where oak grows, consider the qualities of the tree—slow growing, old, shedding, and renewing, and work with the energies of a similar tree in your area.

Before taking your acorns or oak, spend time with the tree and see if this is what is right for it. (I encourage taking from branches or limbs that have fallen. It isn't necessary to cut a living tree unless it's in danger of falling and injuring someone.) If you feel that it is right for the tree to take something from it, a suggested recitation is as follows:

Brigid of the Oaken Grove,
My sacrifice please now behold,
I seek protection, strength, and life,
Oak bar the door from pain and fright.

Do your work, be it collecting trash or another method. The simple act of sacrifice may open the door for greater sacrifices that you are able to make outside of the forest. If the timing seems wrong to collect wood or seed, try again at another time.

MEDITATION: JOURNEY TO THE GROVE

The following meditation is designed to explore personal sacrifices in exchange for manifestation of deeper desires, one's own Will, and identifying sacrifices necessary to make it happen.

Sit quietly with closed eyes and even breathing. Acknowledge the sounds you hear or thoughts that flow through your mind. Try not to fight or follow them. Imagine the dark behind your eyes is a black mist. Imagine you stand on a soft path. Although you cannot see, allow yourself to trust in the dark and to walk forward. You carry a small bag. In time, the mists begin to thin. The full moon and stars begin to appear in the sky above you. You are in a forest. Shortly, you will begin to hear the sound of water, but it is not the ocean. You can hear waves gently lapping against land.

In the distance, you can see the moon's reflection on the water. As the trees thin further, you find yourself at the edge of a great lake. There is just enough light to reveal your reflection on the surface. Sit with your image for a moment.

The waves startle. A boat approaches and gently scrapes against the shore. If the boat seems sturdy enough, climb aboard. The vessel pulls away from the land and heads across the water for the land on the other side, just barely in your sight. The mists have fully settled and the stars shine bright. The land ahead contains a flickering orange dot, passing in and out of sight. As your boat approaches the land, you see that it also is covered with forest, even thicker than before. In the distance, you can hear the sound of a flute playing.

The boat reaches the shore at last and you step out onto land, covered with dried leaves. Clutching your bag, you begin to walk across this new shore, the leaves crunching loudly beneath your feet. Two gallant trees mark a clearing in the forest. Begin walking toward them. Acorns litter the ground as the leaves turn to soil. You recognize the two trees as majestic oak. Pass between them and continue on the path, which gently rises. Past these two trees, you pass another two oaks, larger than the first. In passing those, you pass two more even larger than before, and then two more. The trees create a canopy of rustling leaves above your head. You feel acorns crackle beneath your feet as these ancient trees direct a path through the forest. Continue to walk uphill.

In time, the path will turn gently to your left and continue to rise. The oaks have become enormous, their limbs bowing toward the ground, but their tops so tall they vanish into the night sky. The flickering orange has reappeared. The path between the trees grows wider.

Eventually, the oaks give way to a massive clearing. In the center, a giant fire roars. The clearing is ringed by the largest oaks you have ever seen, their top branches knitted together and their limbs entangled so that you are completely surrounded by tree and leaf. Each trunk has a face all to its own, carved into the trunk. You enter the clearing, still clutching your bag.

Standing by the fire are two figures dressed in fur and hide. A third figure, covered from head to toe in a cloak of fur, stands facing the fire.

This figure turns—it is a woman. The fire behind her creates shadow and you cannot see her face, but only her eyes.

She leads you around the fire. Behind it is an altar. At this time, share with the woman your true Will. What is your true Will? What is it you desire most? Speak your truest Will and do not lie—she will know.

If you are able to articulate your truest Will, tell her then what you are willing to sacrifice to see this Will come to manifest.

Open the bag and inspect what is inside. Decide if you are willing to lay these on the altar, for these things will be sacrificed for your Will to manifest. Are you willing to lay them down?

Then, the woman takes you by the hands and lays you on the altar. Stretched out with the stone slab beneath you and the stars above you, the roaring fires to your side, the woman asks you a question. Answer honestly.

Be present with her as she does her work.

When the work has completed, thank her for any messages, assistance, or otherwise. You exit the circle, traveling back down the path through the oak avenue to the boat. You travel back across the water to the place where you started. The stars fade, the darkness once again becomes the blackness behind your eyes. When you feel you are settled back in your present world once more, open your eyes. Record thoughts in a journal.

Ideally, this meditation would be performed on a full moon and the subsequent ritual performed six days after the following new moon. Some important areas to note include your reflection on the water. It may indicate your soul's current image, although some who do this meditation report it being difficult to see an image. This may happen during a time of change or transformation, or it simply may not be something your mind is in need of grasping. The motion on the water can be indicative of the emotional state: stormy, still, murky, bubbly. If at any point the boat is not seaworthy or if the path is too difficult or even unavailable, it might be best to try the exercise again later. Note also the animal fur. As in the exercise at the start of the book, this may indicate a power animal.

The following ritual can be performed immediately following the meditation. Doing them in tandem will increase the experience for both.

RITUAL: MISTLETOE RITE OF SACRIFICE

Romans wrote that the Druids collected mistletoe on the sixth day following a new moon, cutting the mistletoe from its oak host with a golden sickle. Mistletoe and its miraculous qualities of growth without root often required a sacrifice of importance such as a bull or a human. The herb was considered all-healing, one of the few to keep its berries in winter, and for that reason was believed to cure infertility. Kissing under mistletoe is believed to have derived from this belief. Mistletoe is a good herb to use in personal or group rites requiring sacrifice. It grows directly out of the oak, but despite its seemingly parasitic nature, it is a bedrock of stability for ecosystems, being a primary source of food for animals, and birds in particular. Mistletoe is, however, poisonous to humans and should be used symbolically, never ingested.

Gather the following supplies and perform this rite on the sixth day after a new moon. Due to the need for mistletoe, this rite will most likely be easiest to do during the Christmas season. This ritual is designed for a group, hopefully with at least one person who can drum. It can be performed alone, but you may want to have a recording of a drumbeat playing for extra emphasis.

Materials

Sprigs of mistletoe, one for each person in the rite.

Three red candles.

Brigid oil (see Chapter 10).

A decadent treat and tasty drink. Must be something all parties can agree upon and consume.

Prior to the ritual, perhaps by doing the previous meditation, examine what is blocked. The need for sacrifice does not come from a vacuum. Participants should then write or draw on paper or construct a symbolic image of the habit or thing requiring sacrifice.

Place the red candles and the sprigs of mistletoe on a small table or altar in the center of your working area and cast sacred space in a method familiar to your practices. (See Chapter 10 for a suggested invocation of using Brigid to cast a sacred circle.) Participants should stand outside of the working space.

Once the sacred space has been set, begin the drumbeat and raise energy with the chant: *Brig is come, Brig is welcome ... Brig is come, Brig is welcome.* As the chant continues, one person should approach the space and call out, "O, Oak of Seven Cries! Open the door! O, Oak of Seven Cries! Summon the Brig! O, Oak of Seven Cries! Clear the avenue for the sacrifice is now to begin!" (If you are doing this rite solo, chant until the energy has been raised, and then stop and petition the oak yourself.)

When the energy has risen to a prickly point, each participant should proceed—one at a time—into the sacred space, carrying the paper or effigy of their sacrifice. Each will approach the altar, introducing themselves aloud and announcing their true Will (e.g., "I am Brian! My Will is for a promotion at my job!"). The participant should then anoint himself or herself with the oil, and then step aside for the next person to approach.

After all participants have approached the altar and anointed themselves, the announcing of sacrifice begins. One at a time, each person announces his or her sacrifice. Examples might be: "I sacrifice my time on social media so as to dedicate myself to my best performance at work." "I sacrifice a portion of my salary to charity so that I may give more and heal my heart that suffers." "I sacrifice some gym time so that I may be more helpful at home and improve my marriage." "I sacrifice one night of social outings per week so that I may have more time to rest and focus on me." After all have been declared, whittle each sacrifice down to one or two words and, taking turns, speak the thing that needs sacrifice: "Social media." "Salary portion." "Gym time." "Social outings." Repeat several times, going faster through each round until the energy again has reached a peak point. You may want to experiment with volume levels, if your area allows. If you are doing this work alone, state your sacrifice and immediately transition into the one or two word description.

Some groups may opt to continue chanting for this next section, and some may wish to go silent. Each member takes up their paper and a sprig of mistletoe and, in unison, stabs through the paper with the stem of the plant. Set all papers and mistletoe back on the altar space and leave while the candles burn down. Share the decadent treats and drinks and, if willing, share experiences or thoughts. If doing this work alone, now is the time for reflection and journaling.

Release the sacred space, giving thanks to Brigid and the Spirit of the Oak.

After the rite, participants may want to place their mistletoe sprigs, still through the paper, in their personal ritual space or in another prominent area to be mindful of what they've given up in order for their Will to manifest.

CHAPTER 7

Battle Goddess: Brigid the Warrior

Cath lond Luachra, huasa tuas at chess Brigit, nib firt fas . . .

The fierce battle of Luachra, up above it was seen Brigid, it was no vain miracle . . .

—THE IRISH LIBER HYMNORUM

Early in my Goddess work, I envisioned Brigid as a woman with flaming red hair, brandishing a fiercely shining sword. I was the only one I knew who saw her as such. I was a shrewdly ambitious college student and thought maybe I was seeing the Goddess as I, perhaps arrogantly so, saw myself. Or maybe I was envisioning her in the likeness of determined women in my family, many of whom also had red hair. Pictures of Brigid showed her smiling peacefully and happily by wells or gentle candles. Friends described their encounters with Brigid as a nurturing homemaker, or a gentle muse whispering encouragement toward their creative endeavors. I felt alone in seeing this supposedly gentle Goddess trotting off to war. Why was I seeing her so differently?

Years later, during my first trip to New Orleans, I wanted to find an effigy of Brigid to put on my altar at home. I opened my senses, hoping that Brigid might lead me to that very statue where I could adorn her. I felt "pulled" to take a walk off Bourbon Street, and then another pull to turn again down a windy side road. I followed the pull into an overflowing souvenir store that, unlike so many other stores in NOLA, had nothing to do with magick or the occult. But the pull took me to the back of the store, where it stopped beneath a giant statue of a naked, red-headed woman, posed to lop skulls from skeletons with a chiseled sword. It was perfect for my visions, but also $70 more than what I was able to spend. I later found a similar statue, but a much less expensive one.

A statue believed to depict Brigantia, on display in the Museum of Brittany, Rennes, from the second century B.C.E.

Brigid's warrior aspects are perhaps some of the least familiar, at least in her contemporary worship. When thinking of European War Goddesses, the frequent go-tos included the Morrighan, the Nordic Freya, and certainly the Greek Athena. Brigid is left by the hearthside. While researching this book, I discovered just how true my early visions were to Brigid. Yes, Brigid is a healer, iron-worker, Bard, and overall Patroness of comfort and production. But the warrior was very much a part of who Brigid has been and how she continues to influence and inspire.

WARS OF THE CELTS

Ancient Celtic culture was laced with warfare. Inter-tribal disputes were a regular occurrence, as was defense against invaders from lands north and south. As war was so common, warrior-to-warrior mock-combat was a regular pastime, akin in importance as professional sports are to many contemporary cultures. The practice strengthened the warriors' skills while it entertained the people. In some instances, Kings were chosen for their skills as a warrior, a telling testament to the importance of warfare knowledge in a leader. Their technologically advanced tools and passion for war created a formidable enemy in the Celts to their neighbors. Their peers knew of and wrote about their fierce nature, once described by a contemporary as "brave to the point of foolhardiness."

The Romans, aka Favorite Enemy of the Celts, saw them as a stubborn, unyielding, and horrifying threat. Celtic warriors periodically attacked and pillaged areas of Rome, even as far south as Milan. Posidonius, the Greek philosopher, described the Celtic warriors as "terrifying in appearance, with deep-sounding and very harsh voices." The sight of the invading Celtic warriors, moving south into even the fortress of Rome, caused even seasoned Roman soldiers to flee and vestal virgins to run with the priceless statues of their Goddesses as though they believed their own deities were no match for the Celts and must be protected. The Celts often fought naked except for elaborate torques and, presumably, helmets. The nudity allowed for speed and efficiency, unencumbered by heavy armor. Some believe the Celtic warrior's naked body was a choice to be in full communion with the elements and the Divine. Others say it marked full abandon of fear of pain or death. I once read about a woman who, after a brain injury, physically lost the mental capacity for fear. When a man tried to mug her, the woman's absolute calm caused the potential attacker to flee, her blatant lack of fear inciting all of his. Perhaps this story is a clue to the presence of the Celts on the battlefield: the complete abandon of fear creating full panic in the opposing forces.

For the Celts, war was not a job done solely for the King, Queen, or country—it was a task done for the Gods. War was a religiously inspired practice, woven with ritual and ecstatic prayer. As mentioned in the last chapter, captured enemy prisoners were often sacrificed to the Gods, either in thanksgiving for the Gods' protection or as petition for help in future battles. Even the Celtic Queen Boudica was infamous for her use of such a practice. While the spirited source of Celtic warfare stemmed from collective and personal spiritual devotions certainly aided work on the battlefield, it indirectly led to the Celts' demise. Lacking the organization, structure, or paid soldiers that the Romans had, their southern enemies eventually prevailed through systematic attacks on their region, wearing away at the Celtic stronghold. Despite the passion and drive of the Celtic warriors, even the Celts' weaponry could not adequately replenish the soldiers as they fell or help them properly plan for siege. These conditions, possibly exacerbated by inter-tribal fighting, left the Celts unable to hold against the Roman conquerors in the end.

CELTIC WOMEN, CELTIC WARRIORS

Roman writers wrote about fearing Celtic women more than the men. Whether it was a joke meant to undermine the masculinity of Celtic men or paint a picture of Celtic women being "burly" and therefore, less desirable in the Romans' mindset, it does indicate that Celtic women were known for their strength and prowess, too. They certainly had their own roles in warfare. Romans wrote with flagrant disapproval of the Celts' lack of discrimination based on gender when it came to organizing armies. It's hard to say whether women were actually fighting hand-to-hand combat amongst the men or if they contributed valuable supporting roles. In a period of history when women spent most of their adult lives either pregnant or nursing, it can be assumed that during advanced pregnancy or when nursing infants, they likely stayed away from the front lines, but were still a fundamentally important asset to battle. Elaborate tombs of Warrior-Priestesses indicate that not only did women participate in warfare, they were venerated for it. It is also possible that Priestesses interchanged as warriors more than laywomen did. They were likely pregnant less frequently and much less needed to protect the home and young children. Warrior women juggled many roles. Even the Queen known for warfaring, Boudica, reportedly kept an elaborate and immaculate home during peacetime. Fires needed tending, ale was expected to flow for all guests, and the beds were tightly made with sheepskin and deer hide. War held a place for women, but so did the home.

The mythic story of the final attack on the Druids highlights the Celtic-Priestess warriors. Roman conquerors crossed the Menai Strait to Anglesey Isle, the place known as the nerve center of the Druidic world. Anglesey was home to the major Druid training school. It was also a main provider of food for the region. Conquering this fundamental economic and spiritual epicenter was paramount to the Roman campaign, but it wouldn't be an easy task. The most terrifying aspects of this great battle came from the contribution of the Druidess warrior women.

The story goes that the approaching warriors froze in terror, dropping their oars into the water at the sight on the other side of river. Druids lined the smoke-choked shore and the Druidess warriors wove in and out of the ranks, waving fiery brands, their arms raised toward heaven. They let out shrieking cries so petrifying it stopped the soldiers in their place. Some accounts described the women as naked and streaked with ash, others describe long black robes. The Roman commander urged them not to "quell to the wails of women," his leadership a frail incentive to move toward the frightful sight. The Romans ultimately did advance and despite the fear and the fury, the magick of the Anglesey Druids could not stand against their enemies' swords. The Druids were killed, their groves cut down and altars smashed. With the loss of this island, so came the end of the Druidic stronghold of Celtic Britain. To this day, the shores of the Menai Strait remain an eerie place and a difficult one for even the most skilled engineers to build a bridge across, as though the island continues to shun outsiders.

While this story may not be one to illustrate the success of Druidic warriors, it does give us a clue to the work of the women warriors, particularly in regard to the magick and ritual involved in the fighting. The specifics of these rituals will likely always remain largely mystery, but these stories sketch a portrait of the role of women warriors, and the Celtic Goddesses who towed warrior lines as well.

Menai Strait in Wales.

THE GODDESSES OF WAR

Celtic Goddesses and mythic warrior women were no creatures to cross. While some myths do show women or Goddesses falling prey to attacks or rape by men or enemies, upon reclaiming independence, these mythic characters hurled curses so vengeful the moral of the story remains: "Cross not the Goddess or a woman, for your suffering shall be great." In the mythic story, *The Fate of the Children of Tuireann*, the God Lugh challenges the hero Brian to accomplish many seemingly impossible tasks, not the least of which was procuring a cooking spit from the warrior women of the underworld Island of Fincara where each woman could easily overtake three male warriors on her own. Brian does indeed take the cooking spit, but not through battle, as he could never overtake even a single one of them. Rather, he receives the spit as a gift from the women who were impressed by his bravery and showed him mercy.

The mythic battles frequently relied directly on the prophecies of the Goddesses of war for information to win. As in myths of Brigid's origins, the Dagda could not have won his most important battles without the influence and information from the Morrighan. Later, these Goddesses morphed into fairy-like characters believed to portend war, death, and suffering. The colloquial character of the *Bean sidhe* (banshee), whose shrill scream manifestation of a wailing, inconsolable woman meant death was imminent in a community. This eerie character is thought to be an incarnation of the war and death Goddesses of old.

BRIGID THE WARRIOR

Like the Celtic women, Celtic Goddesses had plenty of work to do that wasn't war-related, but when duty called, they embraced their weapons and joined the fight. Brigid was no different. Even late into her incarnation as a saint, she was one to pick up the fight when the situation called for it.

> As the enemies advanced over the plains of Leinster, the Bishop pleaded to St. Brigid for help. The great saint handed him her staff and screeched a wail that shook the sky and ground, the very sound terrifying the invaders who retreated and fled.
>
> —TRADITIONAL TALE

In the British Celtic world, *Briga* was the Goddess of warfare whose name alone brings warfare back to Brig, the Exalted One. Likewise, the Roman depiction of Brigantia was innately wedded to war, with a spear in hand and helmet. As Roman control settled in and religious attributes began to meld, Brigantia was frequently associated with the Roman Goddess Victoria, or "Victory," just as she was with the Roman Minerva, herself a Goddess of War. Minerva and Brigantia were frequently related to and sometimes even interchanged with the Goddess Sulis, a Goddess known for Brigid-esque qualities such as sun and water, but also for hurling vengeful curses on enemies. Over time, Brigantia's form identified with these two Goddesses until later versions found them practically inseparable. Carvings of Brigantia on Roman forts, in the warrior's helmet and carrying a spear, indicate she was sought for protection even by enemies of the Celts. One such Brigantia statue holds a globe and behind her are wings—both symbols of victory.

Brigid was often regarded as "The Lawmaker." Whether this is a connection to the historical female lawyer called "The Brig" or a transmutation with the lawmaker Goddess Minerva, Brigid's earliest warrior work involved matters of justice. At the Kildare shrine, nine priestesses served as the higher-up of the two-tiered hierarchy. The title for this group of women roughly translated to "Nine Women of Judgments." They served as legal advocates in the region and were believed to advise the High King or Queen at Tara. Both of these tiers, the Nine Women of Judgments and the nineteen tenders of the perpetual flame submitted to the head woman of the order, who always carried the title of Brigid.

The Goddess Brigid's call for battle when justified resonated with her followers far back into antiquity. The historian Plutarch wrote of a Celtic heroine in Gaul named Camma, who was a Priestess of Brigid. Camma was married to a chieftain named Sinatos, who was murdered by a man named Sinorix. Sinorix tried to force Camma to marry him and, in turn, Camma tried to poison her unwanted new husband. Her attempt was thwarted when Sinorix became suspicious of the contents of the wedding chalice, typically shared by the bride and groom at their ceremony. Rather than marry Sinorix, Camma consumed the poison herself and died. This was typical battle move of that era, suicide being a preferred option to capture. This also shows that Brigid's Priestesses were no strangers to subversive means of attack.

How does a Goddess of peaceful aspects such as Healer, Smith, and Bard have a role in warfare, particularly the brutal warfare of the ancient world? This question could be answered with other such questions: To whom do the Bards give praise with songs, yarns, and legends? The fallen Warriors, never forgotten. To whom do the Warriors owe thanks for their weapons and protections? The Smiths who forged the swords and helmets in the forge and on the anvil. Who will the wounded Warriors call for when injured or sick and to whom will the mourning pray when grieving their fallen kin? The Healer who tends the wounds of the living, and the Keener who provides the methods of grief expression. If all that was revered by the Celts found its way to the jurisdiction of the Brig, the Exalted One, Brigid could not be extricated from warfare when her worship base was composed of a culture in which war played a paramount role.

Reflection: What breaks your heart? What sizzles your mind? What, just even the very thought of it, curls your fists and makes you look for your own symbolic (or actual . . .) spear? Is there anything in this world that would prompt you to your battlefield, either literally or figuratively?

In her marriage to Bres, Brigid straddled the dual worlds of opposing sides. Her own son dying in an act of espionage highlights the complexities of warfare, and her own keening at his death reveals the shadow of warfare—beyond the glory comes the suffering. This very keening took place on a battlefield of sorts itself. In other stories, Brigid was the wife of Tuireann rather than Bres and her three sons were named Brian, Iuchar, and Ucharban. Brian slew Cian, the father of Lugh Lamhfhada, who was then assigned the enormous heroic tasks to make up for the loss. War was in Brigid's family, culture, and legacy.

If we consider Brigid's father as the Dagda, she would have inherited magick and healing from him and the ability to raise enough food to literally feed an army, but from her mother the Morrighan she would have attained prophecy and strategy, perhaps even basing her own keening on the cries of the Morrighan's raven. Despite her common guise as the three sisters over the well, the harp, and the anvil, respectively, Brigid was not a Goddess to only stay at home with her fire and well while the rest of the country went to battle. When duty called, she too would pick up the helmet and the spear and do what needed to be done.

This aspect of Brigid did not end during the Irish conversion to Christianity. St. Brigid was known to scream and fly across battlefields to defend the province of Leinster against its enemies, or hand off her staff to a Bishop as indicated previously, traits known to the most brutal of the Celtic War Goddesses. Brigid could command the weather and water, as well as summon animals to rally for her people. In many stained-glass window images, Brigid holds a sword. This was part of a myth in which the young saint's father gave her a jeweled sword to hold for him while he conducted some business, which she immediately gave to a poor beggar passing by, a symbol of the character's ruthless battle on behalf of the poor. The province of Leinster was her main area to protect, but Brigid was believed to travel around Ireland, protecting its people wherever she went. Of a less violent nature, Brigid was known for fearlessly challenging authority, using tricks and magick to win her battles.

One day Brigid went to the Bishop to ask for a plot of land on which to build her abbey at which she would feed the poor, give shelter, and educate the young. The Bishop refused, but still she asked again and again. Finally, the Bishop agreed to grant her the land, but only so much as her cloak would cover, sneering in spite of his own cleverness, but his grin was not for long. Brigid called to her two sisters and the three of them began to unfold her green cloak. Fold after fold, the cloak stretched and stretched until it covered so much land that the Bishop could not see to the end of it. He pleaded for her to stop lest she cover all of Ireland, and granted her the space to build the abbey.

—Traditional tale

And another story . . .

Another time Brigid went to the Bishop for help, this time that he might come and mark out her city for her. They came to the place in which Kildare stands today. At that time a very rich man happened to come along with a hundred horse loads of peeled rods, over the midst of Kildare. These rods would build the start of the city. He had so many while Brigid and her nuns needed so very few. Brigid sent her sisters to ask for a mite few of the rods. They would even take the weakest and oldest of the lot, but their request was refused. The rich man scoffed and continued on down the road. Just outside of Kildare, the horses straightaway sank to their knees in the mud. The horses would not rise again until the man had offered all of the loads of building material to Brigid. Weeping, he did. From these were built St. Brigid's great church in Kildare, and it was the same rich man that fed the workers and paid them their wages.

—Traditional tale

Brigid is a recurrent champion of women. In some stories, St. Brigid helped the Virgin Mary flee with the Christ child into Egypt away from King Herod, who meant to kill him. Brigid placed a bright headdress of lighted candles on her own head, distracting the pursuing soldiers while the mother and child fled. An odd little story about Brigid being the inventor of whistling is believed to have been her gift to women to protect themselves, whistling if they were in danger of being sexually assaulted. As the beacon of ultimate power of the Feminine Divine, Brigid stands as a source of strength for women, particularly in times of duress. Even in Catholic stories, which may frequently depict the ideal qualities of women to be demure and submissive, Brigid's power is revered for her fights for women against oppressive forces.

> *Brigid's sisters walked along, going about their day, when they reached the rushing river where stood a small legion of men on horseback from Connacht and UíNéill, old-time enemies of Leinster. Hoping for a passing kindness, the women asked for their assistance in crossing the river, which was quite rough even in the calmest of times, and the river's temperament that day was not calm at all. The soldiers refused to help the women. Back at the abbey, Brigid heard her sisters' cries for help and in her fury at the injustice, she summoned the waters of the mighty river which instantly rose above the soldiers' heads, drowning them and their horses. Somehow, Brigid's sisters waded across the river to the other side—the water never rising above their knees and the current as gentle as a summer's trickle.*
>
> —INSPIRED BY TRADITIONAL TALE

Activists, lawyers, law-enforcement officials, or anyone working for a sense of justice will find their actions strengthened and empowered by including Brigid magick and ritual prior to engaging in their work. Brigid the Warrior can evoke the image of a mother grabbing a rifle against a dangerous animal or intruder. She's not an energy that attacks, but rather one that defends or rights a wrong in a situation. This is how I personally knew Brigid, in my times as a warrior in my own right. I volunteered as a chaplain during Occupy Wall Street and the stress and suffering downtown was great. Weekly or sometimes daily protests landed people in jail—some were friends of mine, some strangers, and some well-known activists whom I admired. Later, I became involved in anti-fracking movements, trying to keep hydrofracked gas out of the city I live in and love. Because of personal obligations including being my home's primary bread-winner, I could not risk arrest myself even if some of the actions (protesting banks who funded oil and gas companies, for example) were strongly in line with my personal beliefs. In short, I needed to keep the fire burning in the hearth at home, but I lent my aid through chaplaincy and jail support for those who were arrested. I channeled Brigid's Celtic Warrior Woman nature to help me walk in both worlds, that of the home and that of the contemporary battlefield.

Because her primary attributes are of the more domesticated sort, Brigid is primarily a peace-time Goddess. Yet, she fights when provoked. She best not to be called upon as a Goddess of offense tactics, but rather summoned when some sort of battle seems inevitable (I hope I don't need to explain this, but as a PSA of sorts—if you are dealing with a serious bodily, emotional, or other sort of threat, seek help from a professional source.) Also, true to her calling, Brigid is best used against forces that are much bigger than the person summoning them. As she managed to frighten off enemies with the psychological tactics of screeching or in tricking the Bishop by extending her cloak, winning a battle with the help of Brigid is more likely to come through craft and cunning rather than storm and force. However, as with any Deity, expect the unexpected, particularly when asking for help of this nature. She should not be confused with the Morrighan. Although their connections are clear, the Morrighan represents the primal, driving force behind warfare while Brigid represents defense, picking battles, and strategy. If the Morrighan is the "how-to" of battle, Brigid is the "when-to."

MEDITATION: DEFINE YOUR BATTLE

Create a quiet space. If you are able, set your space with a lit candle and a bowl of water—Brigid's flame to guide you and her well to nourish your spirit. Sit with your eyes closed and breathe. Focus on the darkness behind your closed lids, envisioning the blackness to soften into dark mist. Begin to chant softly to yourself: *"Brig, Brig, Brigitta . . . Brig, Brig, Brigitta . . . "*

Envision that you are floating downward, in a gentle spiral. Continue the chant quietly.

In time, you will gently touch ground.

You are standing at the start of a great hallway, and a soft point of light becomes visible before you. You hear the clink of the hammer on the iron anvil. As you approach, the light grows brighter, the gold and green fires of the Forge. You can see Brigid pounding something, shaping an object on a giant anvil in front of a large door. It is a weapon. She lifts it from the anvil and hands it to you. Most of it glows red-hot, but part of it is cool enough that you are able to hold it with no issue. Brigid at the Forge will ask you a question. If you are able to answer, you then cross through the door and continue down the hallway. The walls are lit with torches to guide your way. Your weapon's edge still glows with the heat from the forge, but is comfortable in your hand.

You hear gentle splashing of water, as though someone is washing. The torches reflect a glimmer of water farther down the hall. As you approach, you see Brigid gently churning the waters of her well. Another set of doors are behind her. She looks up and sees you. Take your still-glowing weapon and plunge it into the water. Watch the images that rise in the steam. Brigid at the Well will ask you a question. If you are able to answer, walk past her through the next set of doors.

Behind the next set is a large chamber, warmly lit by more torches than the hallway. On the walls, great portraits of warriors are displayed. Who are these warriors? Why are they here?

A sudden wind bursts through the chamber as two doors open into the outdoors. It is dawn, and the light is soft in the sky. As you walk out the doors onto the landscape, you realize you are standing on a long-forgotten battlefield. What lies on this battlefield?

Brigid calls your name from behind you. You turn to see her, wearing her helmet for battle. In one hand, she holds a sharp spear. In the other hand, she holds the round globe of victory. Ask her one question. Listen for her answer. Whether or not she answers you, Brigid holds the globe toward you. In it, you will see something. Watch the globe.

When your time with Brigid has concluded, you thank her as the Smith, the Healer, and as the Warrior. The light of the battlefield fades. You see nothing but the black mist once more. Traveling upward, upward, upward to where you began. When you feel your feet and body once more in your present life, open your eyes.

Record images and thoughts in a journal.

RITUAL: A RITUAL FOR WARRIOR BRIGID

If your journey brings you to a place where you need extra support from warrior-type energy, the following rite can help. This is intended for strength when working against seemingly oppressive forces, such as a court case, rally, or protest, but can also be channeled for things of less intensity, such as problems at work or conflict among family members. If you do not have a pressing issue, but would simply like to experience some of the energy of Brigid the Warrior, this rite is a good introduction. The intention is to give the practitioner the strength to stand his or her ground, proceed with action for the highest good, and strengthen defenses. The saying included is adapted from a Christian prayer to St. Brigid. As always, this ritual should never be a substitute for legal action or protection in the event of emotional or physical abuse. Seek professional help or legal assistance.

Set your ritual table or space with a red cloth and a gold or yellow candle. As always, placing items representative of your struggle (photos or a written description of the issue) are valuable in sending the necessary energy to the right place.

If your practice or tradition utilizes a sword or athame (ritual knife), have it ready for this working. If you do not have one of these, a kitchen knife will do just fine. Consecrate the tool with salt water and incense and declare its intention for use in this rite. Trace a circle around your ritual space, envisioning white-gold light coming from the tip of the blade. You may opt to use the Circle Casting listed in Chapter 10. If you are working with a group or a partner and either you or they have access to a drum, a steady drumbeat akin to a battle-call will be helpful to set the tone. Utilizing acorns or oak are also helpful energies for bringing about strength.

Light the candle and chant *"Brig is come! Brig is welcome!"* until you feel the energy rise in the room, which should come about like a pricking on the skin or perhaps raising of hairs on the back of your neck.

Say the following with power and conviction. Do not be afraid to raise your voice if you are able. If you are working with a group, call and response affirming the declaration is helpful such as *"I shall not be slain!"* or *"He/She/They shall not be slain!"*

The Blessing of Brigid be upon me!
Each day and each night
The Descent of Brigid be true,
I shall not be slain,
I shall not be harmed,
I shall not be confined,
I shall not be torn apart,
I shall not be trodden down,
I shall not be afraid,
I shall not be cast aside,
Brigid protect me,
Brigid allows me to see,
Brigid, wrap me in your green mantle,
Brigid, stand beside me with spear,
I shall not be forgotten,
No fire shall burn me,
No sun shall burn me,
No moon shall blanch me,
No water shall drown me,
No flood shall drown me,
No tricks shall distract me,
No earthly being destroy me.

If you have a specific issue that requires Brigid's assistance, this is the time to describe it in detail. Be specific about what assistance you may need in your situation.

Whether or not you have a specific need or simply want Brigid's energy for warrior presence, say aloud, *"Fortify me with your spear and defend me with your shield. I am of Brigid the Warrior. The Warrior Brigid is of me."*

Repeat the text above one final time. Sit with the energies of the space and envision all white-gold light you've surrounded the room with returning and enveloping you. This is Brigid's Warrior energy seeping into your form. Let the candle burn down as much as you are able. Record any thoughts that come to you.

To offer thanks for this rite, find the grave of a veteran soldier and pray for their spirit, being sure to thank them for the time they gave as a warrior.

CHAPTER 8

Imbolc:
Brigid the Springtime
Goddess, the Mother,
and the Midwife

This statue of Brigid with the children is located on the grounds of St. Brigid's Church in Suncroft Village, just a few miles away from Kildaretown. Photo courtesy of Elizabeth Guerra-Walker.

One February 1, several years before I wrote this, I hosted a small gathering of friends in my tiny living room to celebrate Brigid's holiday: Imbolc. The memory of that cold night, my guests cramped up in a tight circle, is now a signpost in my crazy journey that says, "Here's where things took a serious turn." Unbeknownst to me, this impromptu collection of curious friends would blossom into the community I would lead and learn from for years afterward. The ritual itself wasn't even the most memorable part of the evening. A close friend who attended that night's rite found out earlier in the day that she was pregnant. She also volunteered to divine the future for us, traditional for an Imbolc rite, and went into a deep trance. After shouting at me, "Where is my book???? Where is my book???," she then cried out, "Your Seer fights me . . . I shall leave her two!" When my friend came out of trance, she remembered nothing else aside from the number two. When we told her what she had said while in trance, she admitted that Brigid's presence had been overwhelming and she tried to push her away. An image of Brigid came up before her, waving two fingers and flashing a wicked smile. A couple of months later, she learned she was indeed carrying "two." Although my friend has dark hair and eyes, her red-haired and green-eyed twin girls were born later that year.

HOLIDAYS OF THE CELTS

Imbolc, Brigid's holiday, is indeed a time of magick and synchronicity. Although the days technically grow longer after the Winter Solstice, it isn't until early February (or August, if you are in the Southern Hemisphere) that this change is noticeable. In the ancient Celtic world, the lengthening of days meant far more than warmer days and later sunsets. It was a sign that the most dangerous point of the year had passed. Winter was a time of illness, hunger, and death. Although the ground was cold and often the snow still present, the first stirrings of spring arrived with Imbolc, and with them, the promise of health, food, and life restored again.

Celtic holidays marked the turns in the agricultural cycle. Druids, as the keepers of time, were the curators and preservationists of these traditions and rites. The great fire rites at these holidays stood as the main points in the circle of the year. The following descriptions illustrate practices in Celtic Ireland, but different versions of these rites were found all over Celtic Europe. Bealtaine, in early May, was the beginning of summer. Cattle were driven to pasture and rites of fertility took place. It was the optimal time for would-be mothers to conceive. Lughnasadh, at the beginning of August, focused on the harvest Goddess Tailtu's sacrifice of clearing the forest for the corn and crops to grow. A series of games akin to the Greek Olympic games was held in honor of Tailtu and the first collection of harvest produce. Samhain, in early November, marked the end of the harvest season. All field goods had to be collected before the frosts would set in. It was the last point of bountiful fresh food for the year and also a time of death. Cattle not fit to last the winter were slaughtered for food and to preserve resources for healthier livestock. Imbolc was celebrated roughly around dates now called January 31 through February 1, as Celtic holidays were celebrated from sundown to sundown. Imbolc was marked by the time when the cows and sheep would begin lactating again, the first signs that winter was on its way out of the land. The milk products would have been some of the first items of fresh food the people would have had since early November. Women who conceived at Bealtaine delivered their babies around this time. The world was coming back to life. Through the lens of the harvest, Samhain was an end. Imbolc was a beginning.

SIGNIFICANCE OF IMBOLC TO THE CELTS

Early February may seem like a very early spring to much of the Northern Hemisphere, particularly in northwestern Europe. Yet roughly 7,000 years ago, the climate of the Celtic region was much more akin to the contemporary Mediterranean region. February 1 was likely a much warmer time, one suitable for crop planting. If this is the case, the significance of the Imbolc holiday may be as old as the Boreal Period, which took place 7000–5000 B.C.E.

In the United States, February 2 is Groundhog Day, marking the return of the furry little animal from its underground bunker, which is one of North America's first signs that the winter is going to end. In Europe, the earliest signs of spring included the snakes arising from the ground (in areas other than Ireland where snakes have never inhabited), or animals coming out of hibernation. For the Celts, the most important sign of Imbolc was the lactation of the cattle and sheep. The word "Imbolc" derives directly from *Imbolg* or *Oimelc,* words meaning "of milk" or "in the belly." Celtic economy was heavily based on farming, and dairy products were a main food staple. The role of ewes and cattle production was so important to the functionality of the community that the entire agricultural system and important aspects of the religion centered on their ability to produce. The change in the Earth Mother, while she could be brutal during the tenuous parts of the harvest and dangerously unforgiving in the winter, was most welcome in her springtime form. Brigid the Exalted, who was given Imbolc as her Patron holiday, indicates that this may have been the most important point in the Celtic year and certainly the most beloved.

BRIGID: GODDESS OF SPRINGTIME AND THE SACRED MOTHER

When the land darkens at Samhain, when the veils between this world and the Spirit are at their very thinnest, the Cailleach, the Old Hag of Winter who destroys all and brings darkness to the

land, kidnaps Brigid from her place at the great Harvest Fires
and whisks her across the chilling landscape. She stows Bright
Brigid away in her Hag's fortress of Ben Nevis. There she remains,
a prisoner of winter until Imbolc eve. At this time, Brigid's brother
Oenghus, the God of Eternal Youth, will ride from the Otherworld
on a white horse to rescue her each Imbolc eve. On her release,
the icy Hag chases the pair across the landscape, raising great
storms to thwart their escape. Brigid pushes back against the old
Hag with her fiery arrows of the sun, and turns the Cailleach back
to stone. The light returns, the cows give milk, and the new babies
cry. Spring once again returns to the land, and so it continues
each Imbolc from now until the end of time.

—Inspired by traditional tale

Like the Grecian myth of Persephone and Hades, the space between Samhain and Imbolc is Brigid's own journey into the Shadow world. The earth is quiet, cold, and resting. This myth, in various forms, may be thousands of years old. *Brig* as "The Lady of Springtime," is the spirit of the early spring whose rule alternates with that of a wintertime Goddess. Cailleach may simply mean "old woman" as in Old Woman of Winter, the way other vernacular refers to the cold months as "Old Man Winter." Depending on the location, the Cailleach was associated with natural wisdom, perhaps the storytelling by the fires, harvesting, and preservation, but also wild and wicked storms that would ravage the land every year.

Other myths talk of Brigid as both herself and the Cailleach, having two faces—one being young and comely, the other old and haggard. At Imbolc, the Cailleach, transforms into Brigid by drinking from a sacred spring before dawn:

On the eve of Imbolc, the icy Winter Hag, the Cailleach, travels
to the forest of a mystical island, where within lies the Well of

Eternal Youth. At dawn's first light, the frigid Goddess drinks the water that bubbles in a crevice of a rock, and is transformed into Brigid, the Goddess of Spring and life who strikes a white wand upon the earth to make it green again.

—Traditional tale

Still other myths describe Brigid as dipping a white wand or breathing life into the mouth of winter, waking the sleeping earth, and bringing tears to Winter's eyes (a symbol of the thaw), and ushering along the sounds of spring. The white wand may be a stick of birch, or it could be a symbol of the blinding late winter sun. Some stories say that cold trembles for its safety on Imbolc and flees for its life on St. Patrick's Day in mid-March, as spring firmly takes hold:

Bride put her finger in the river
on the Feast Day of Bride,
and away went the hatching mother of the cold.
And she bathed her palms in the river
on the Feast Day of Patrick,
and away went to the conception of the mother of cold.

—Alexander Carmichael

Like the forge's fire or the energy welling up from the Bard's song, Brigid the Spring Goddess breathes life back into the cold, sleeping land. Like the Forge, the Wells, or the Bard's abilities, Imbolc reflected magick. It marked the tide of easier, gentler days to come when planting was possible and food was plentiful. True to her nature as *Fiery Arrow*, the sun that seems to abandon the world for a time gently returns to stir the sleeping and warm the frozen ground. Streams and wells will soon begin to trickle, their healing powers abundant once again.

Brigid has also been described in relation to the different cycles as the Earth Mother. At Bealtaine, she is a young woman on the threshold of marriage with the elements. At Lughnasadh, she produces the harvest. Come Samhain, she assumes the form of the Winter Hag, but at Imbolc she is the infant Goddess born again. Be it title, name, or season, Brigid is most powerful at the start of spring. In another version of the Threshold Rites, a sheaf of wheat from the Samhain harvest was placed outside doors of homes on the eve of January 31. Some believed that the Goddess was present in the sheaf in her winter Cailleach form. Upon Imbolc, the sheaf becomes the infant Goddess Brigid once again, marking the fragile beginnings of the new agricultural cycle. When sowing time comes again, the grain from the final sheaf was then mixed with the new seed, to nurture the earth again, encouraging the next harvest, and ensuring a cycle of life and rebirth.

She who put beam in moon and sun,
She who put food in earth and herd,
She who put fish in stream and sea,
Hasten the butter up to me.
Pray Brigid, see my children yonder,
Waiting for buttered buns,
White and yellow.

—TRADITIONAL IRISH PRAYER FOR IMBOLC

In the Threshold Rites, the old harvest was dismembered to become the new harvest, the protector, and the domestic helper. Other rites called *Brídeog* included the human-shaped fixture of rushes, sometimes dressed as a young girl. The *Brídeog* was carried from house to house by a procession to bless the entire community and collect money for charity or the local church. These were Catholic rites conducted in honor of St. Brigid, but the connection to the Harvest Goddess and the Earth Goddess born again is unmistakable.

In a pantheon of so many harsh characters, it's curious to come across one who is as gentle as Brigid, at least in the light that Imbolc paints her. At Imbolc, Brigid is the calming voice that says, "It's okay to come out, now!" Just as her power infused previously raw ore into invaluable tools, so does her return at Imbolc transform a barren world into one fruitful and bountiful. She is the Smith on the land, heating the cold soil to life again. She is the Bard that entices the birds to song and the Well that brings health and renewal to the people. The ancient Celts knew the Earth Mother could be wicked and cruel. Perhaps they saw Imbolc as a time when she could also be kind.

BRIGID: THE SACRED MIDWIFE

Brigid's aunt, Fainche, had very long been barren and came to Brigid for a miracle. Brigid fasted three days in the church at Kildare and an angel came and said to her: "O Holy Brigid, bless thy aunt's womb and she will bring forth a distinguished son." Brigid ran to her aunt and prayed vigilantly over her womb, until Fainche felt the miracle stir within her. Fainche had a son that year, Colmán, and went on to have a further three: Conall, Eogan, and Cairpre.

—Traditional tale

Early spring is not always kind. The rain, sleet, and mud are the byproducts of transformation into spring. But Imbolc and its rites are a reminder that gentler days are just around the corner. Likewise, motherhood may be sometimes imagined as a peaceful existence. The image of a quiet mother rocking a sleeping baby is the ideal and certainly a piece of the picture, but the whole embodiment is wrought with work, fragmented sleep, and worry for the children. The process of the early days of spring, like birth, is tumultuous. Fluctuating weather patterns, thaws that bring floods, and storms brought by the mix of warming air on a cold world are a normal part of the Imbolc process. Still, this period of the year was optimal for the Celtic birthrate. Pregnancies begun at Bealtaine allowed for the mothers to work through the pivotal harvest season. They would experience the least mobile part of their pregnancy during the darkest months of the year, when there was less work to be done and the community could collectively focus on rest. Birthing in early February, in time with the return of the dairy products, would mean well-nourished mothers and babies could thrive better in the warmer months, cared for by communities with access to the most plentiful food sources.

Fertility Goddesses were most often honored at springtime shrines, the mysteries of birth combined with the abundant earth vital to life. Later, when the shrines supported the Roman Gods, nursing mothers wore amulets of the Goddess Sulis, who was frequently interchanged with Brigantia, to encourage lactation. Perhaps because of the springtime connection, and because of the earth once again producing, Brigid became synonymous with motherhood—both in having her own children with Bres and becoming the midwife, literally ushering new life into the world.

Brigid's father, Dubthach, the Chieftain of Leinster, drove his chariot along the road with his bondmaid, Broicsech, who would one day become the mother of Brigid. They passed and stopped inside the house of the Druid Mathghean who, during their visit, prophesied that the bondmaid would give birth to a child of great renown. In hearing this story, Dubhthach's wife became enraged with jealousy and sold the bondmaid to a Bard who in turn then sold her to a Druid of Tirconnell. By this time, Broicsech was heavily pregnant with Brigid. This Druid gave a great feast to which he invited the King of Conaill whose wife was also expecting a child. The Druid foretold that the child would be born at sunrise the next day, and neither within the house nor without and would be greater than any other child in Ireland.

That night the Queen gave birth, but her child was dead. At sunrise the bondmaid, Broicsech, bore a child while standing with one foot inside the house and the other outside of it. Broicsech's child was then brought into the presence of the Queen's child who, miraculously, was restored to life. This Druid travelled with Broicsech and her baby into Connacht when, in a dream, he saw "Three clerics in shining garments," who poured oil on the girl's head and thus completed the order of baptism in the usual manner, calling the child Brigid.

—TRADITIONAL TALE

This Christian myth of St. Brigid summons Brigid's roots as a springtime Goddess. Even the King and Queen, the sovereign beings of the land, were not immune to the tides of death. Their child, symbolizing the new harvest, is without life until the presence of the infant Brigid, the fledgling Spring Goddess, breathes life anew. Brigid's mother, straddling the doorway as she gives birth, is a reminder of Brigid's place in both the spring world of the living, and the winter realm of the dead. In the final part of this myth, three clerics, similar to the wise men visiting the infant Jesus, reveal Brigid's level of importance to Celtic faith, even in the transfer to Christianity. Like Jesus, whose presence in the Christian faith restores the world, Brigid is renowned and prophesied light and life to the world, but through her embodiment of the awakened earth.

While her Celtic Goddess myths reveal her as a mother herself of three sons, St. Brigid was most often a midwife or a foster mother to Jesus. This may be in line with some Christian theologies that put sanctity on the idea of a Virgin, which would be rendered impossible for Brigid had she been a mother herself, as only the Virgin Mary could give birth without having had intercourse. The midwife secured Brigid's legacy as a fertility being. In addition, she was also considered the midwife to the Christ child's birth and, in some stories, even his foster mother. In the myths from this region, the role of the foster mother was on par with (and in some cases surpassed) the birth-mother role in importance. The idea of the Irish St. Brigid being a midwife in a story based in the Middle East may seem rather absurd, but this was a way in which the exalted Goddess would carve her way in the new religion as Christianity settled in, taking no less than the most important place next to the most important character in the new religion.

Brigid was a daughter of poor parents. She worked as a serving maid at a tiny inn at the tiny town of Bethlehem. It was a torrid time—a great drought had struck the land. The master of the inn went away with his cart to get water from a far distance, entrusting Brigid to watch the inn. He left her a serving of water and portion of bread to tide her over until his return. Because of its scarcity, the master ordered Brigid to share no food or drink to anyone and to not extend shelter until he returned with provisions.

Not long after the master left, two strangers came to the door and asked for a place to stay for the night. They were hungry and weary and in desperate need of water. The woman was heavily pregnant and while Brigid could not risk giving them shelter, gave them her bread and water. The couple ate at her doorway, thanked her kindly, and went along their way.

Brigid was saddened at the couple's condition—particularly for the young woman in her time of need, and regretted she could not give them shelter from the heat or any more water or food than what she gave them. Out of concern for the couple, she ran out into the late afternoon sun and pursued them for hours, until it was very dark. Just then, she saw a golden light shining from a stable door. She ran to the stable and saw the woman, who was the Virgin Mother, about to give birth. Brigid aided the woman, delivering the child who was Jesus the Christ, the son of God who had come to Earth, and the couple was Joseph and Mary. Brigid put three drops of water from a nearby spring of pure water on the baby's forehead in the name of God. The world rejoiced and it is because of this that Brigid is known as the Aid-Woman of Mary or Foster Mother of Christ. Still others call her the Godmother of the Son of God and yet others call her the Godmother of Jesus Christ of the Bindings and Blessings. Christ himself is known as the Foster Son of Bride, the Foster Son of the Bride of the Blessings, and sometimes even the Little Fosterling of Brigid.

—Traditional tale

Few saints would be able to get away with being credited for delivering or even rearing the Christ child as the Foster-Mother title would suggest. More remarkable still is that the baby Jesus could possibly be titled the "Little Fosterling of Brigid," which insinuates a greater power credited to Brigid than even the Son of God, himself. There may be a cultural history component to this telling. As the midwife ushers the new babies into the world, Brigid the midwife ushered the new religion into the land.

Reflection: Change is necessary. All things must grow and adapt or else perish. This is how our vulnerable species survived over hundreds of thousands of years. Likewise, we as individuals must adapt to cultural shifts and changes in our own lives or face death within ourselves. When changes are imminent and uncomfortable, like the discomfort in the early time of spring, how can we adapt ourselves so that we too can grow? If Brigid can adapt from the Earth Goddess in her indigenous religion to the Exalted Foster Mother of the Great God of the New Religion, what roles can we carve for ourselves when great and unavoidable changes take place around us?

BRIGID AT THE BEDSIDE OF THE MOTHERS

Brigid's aid was summoned by laboring mothers when their delivery time was near. In areas of Scotland, Brigid was petitioned as the Woman on her Knees, or *"It was Bride fair who went on her knee,"* describing the midwife's position when assisting at a birth. In the Scottish Highlands and Hebrides, it was once traditional for women to give birth while kneeling on one knee. At the same time, the midwife or a midwife's assistant would stand on the doorstep with her hands on the door jambs and softly speak the following:

Bride! Bride! Come in,
Thy welcome is truly made,
Give thou relief to the woman,
And give the conception to the Trinity . . .

The mother might appeal directly to Brigid, herself:

There came to me assistance,
Mary fair and Bride;
As Anna bore Mary,
Mary bore Christ,

As Eile bore John the Baptist
Without flaw in him,
Aid thou me in mine unbearing,
Aid me, O Bride!
As Christ conceived of Mary
Full perfect on every hand,
Assist thou me, foster mother
The conception to bring from the bone;
And as thou did'st aid the Virgin of joy,
Without gold, without corn, without kine,
Aid thou me, great is my sickness,
Aid me, O Bride!

Logically, the doorway of the home makes sense for a birthing mother. The position of being on the knee allows for gravity to bring the child into the proper birthing position, and the doorway could be used as support to keep the mother upright. Perhaps for this reason, the threshold of the home was a sacred place. Symbolically, it represented the sometimes perilous threshold between death and birth. Imbolc Brigid not only brought the light back to the world at the springtime, she brought in human life into the world often at this same time of year, ushering women and children through the potential dangers of the threshold of birth.

TRADITIONAL RITES OF IMBOLC

While researching this book, I came across enough Imbolc traditions to fill a tome. In the early twentieth century, the Irish Folklore Commission issued a questionnaire about the various rites called *The Feast of St. Brigid* in an attempt to record the traditions. The results filled nearly 2,500 pages of manuscript, marking Brigid as a saint whose range, number of customs, and stories numbered greater than nearly any other saint. These few paragraphs are merely a scratch on the tip of that Brigid iceberg. But if one could find a single word to encapsulate these practices, it would be "Welcome," Imbolc welcomes Brigid and, through her, welcomes light, spring, and life.

Like a female Santa Claus, Brigid was believed to visit all the houses on Imbolc eve. When it was time to turn in for the night, the hearth ashes would be spread delicately and smoothly over the coals. The ashes were meant to be Brigid's bed, hopefully comfortable enough to suit her liking and earn her blessing when she would come through to lie down to bed for the night. If the ash carried imprints the next morning, Brigid had blessed the house. If the ashes had been found undisturbed, then Brigid had skipped the house and misfortune may be present. A sacrifice, such as the chicken blood at the crossroads, might have been necessary to re-earn her favor.

Another Brigid Imbolc rite involved a silk ribbon or a cord. On Imbolc eve, such a piece would be measured and placed outside, either on the threshold or windowsill. Come the next morning, the piece would be measured again. If it were deemed longer in the morning than the night before, luck would come about over the course of the following year. If it had seemed to shrink, misfortune was evident. The idea was that Brigid had blessed the ribbons when she passed, causing them to lengthen. As in the ashes, if the cord did not grow or had seemed to shrink, Brigid was displeased. Blessed cords or ribbons were ever after preserved as healing amulets, particularly as headache remedies.

One beautiful story I read involved an old woman who lived in a remote area of Ireland in the nineteenth century. She owned a shawl that she had treated as a Brigid ribbon for fourteen years. She claimed that any time she requested something of the shawl, it was granted by the grace of St. Brigid. One such story was about a time her cow struggled in labor. The calf wouldn't come. It took several men to hold the cow down to assist, yet the calf would not budge. After hours of watching the cow labor, fearful for the life of the calf and its mother, the woman fetched her shawl and shook it over the cow. She then went onto her knees and prayed fiercely to Brigid. Ten minutes later, she claimed, the calf finally came through. Both mother and calf were fine. The woman later shook her shawl over a childless woman who desperately wanted a family, and soon after the woman had a child.

In some areas of Ireland, a little wooden branch was burned in a domestic fire on Imbolc eve. When the fire was quenched, a soot cross was marked with it on the arms of family members. This may have similar resonance to the burning sacrifices of millennia prior, but its later meanings were certainly connected to life and growth. Fires at Imbolc had significant associations with fertility as well. Ashes from local fires were strewn upon the fields. This act was vital in enhancing fertility of crops, in both a ritualistic and practical context. The intent was Brigid's blessing, which might have manifested through the ash enriching the soil. Likewise, fertility of livestock would have been of dire importance. Imbolc was also a time in which cows, sheep, or other livestock were blessed in protective rites. The Brigid who served as the first abbess of Kildare, formerly a Chief Druidess, was probably involved in ceremonies to invoke Divine help in the blessings of crops, animals, and certainly human mothers as well.

THE ST. BRIGID'S CROSS

Brigid walked along the road one day and heard a low, suffering moan from a hut. She followed the sound and entered. There she found a dying tribal chieftain, still devoted to the Gods of Old.

Brigid told him of her conversion to the new faith of Christianity and wished to share the powers of her new God with the dying man who otherwise was quite alone in his last moments. The dying man would not listen and insisted she seek a Druid to come to his aid. Brigid knew there were no Druids left within a two-day ride. The ailing chieftain would die without a word spoken in honor of his spirit, no rites performed in honor of his death. She sat with the man in silence for many hours, dabbing his brow, holding his hand, trying to offer some comfort. The chieftain began to despair. Would there be no one to speak to the Gods of the Sun and the Water or the Spirits of the hills to notify them of his passing? Would he walk the earth for all time as a wailing, confused ghost? As the sun set and the chieftain's breathing thickened and weakened, Brigid ran across the dusky hillside and desperately pulled up rushes, weaving them into a hasty cross. She hurried back to the hut, showing the cross to the chieftain, and described the sacrifice her new God Christ had made and the eternal life He offered after death. In his last waning moments, the old chieftain recognized the Gods of the Sun in the sun-shaped rush cross, felt the soothing River Goddess in the description of Christ's healing. He knew the sacrificed Christ was the same as the slain Corn Gods of all the Harvest Rites he had ever known. Through Brigid's Christian rite, his soul would know peace and eternal reunion with all those who had gone before him. He allowed her to pray to her God for his soul, and sing a sweet hymn. He clutched the reed cross until life left his body, and when the time came for his burial it remained pinched between his fingers.

—INSPIRED BY TRADITIONAL TALE

I did expand upon this common myth of St. Brigid and the construction of the St. Brigid's cross. Like many Christian stories, it involved a last-minute conversion of a dying person after simply laying their eyes upon the symbol of Christ. Even as a Christian child, I had a hard time wrapping my mind around these stories—how could a simple shape with barely an explanation cause such great change in a person's heart? Now, as a Neo-Pagan, I appreciate the story of St. Brigid and the Pagan Chieftain as a reminder that we can change the world with only what we have at our fingertips. In telling it for this book, I sat deeper with what might have been going on during the time of the chieftain's passing, why he might have been open to accepting the new faith at the last moments, and what he could have seen in the cross that gave him so much comfort. I also sat with Brigid's compassion and her relentless resolve to be there for the man in his last moments alive.

Reflection: Look all around you. What could you use, within your grasp, that could change the world? For me, it's my computer to write these words. It is also my phone to call someone and let them know they are loved. It is my window, which I can wave through to passersby on the street. What is available to you, right now, that you could use to change the world?

The St. Brigid's cross is a prevalent image in contemporary Celtic Christianity and evermore a fixture in the Neo-Pagan revival. It is traditionally made from rushes, although it is quite easy to find representations in other forms. I wear a pewter cross and our home has a brass cross in the entryway. Traditionally, the rush crosses were picked—not cut—on Imbolc eve. In some areas, the person gathered the material for the crosses in secret. Sometimes, rushes were collected by a group of people, the gatherers praying quietly to themselves without speaking to one another until they reached home. Rushes might be kept from Palm Sunday (taking place the Sunday before Easter) and woven into crosses at Imbolc of the following year. Sometimes, the maker might insert grains of corn between the rushes.

The cross's shape is believed to be a derivative of sun symbolism, its very nature hinting at Pagan roots. The four equal points are slightly off center, which gives the eye the illusion that the cross could turn of its own volition, and speaks to the turn of the seasons and sun's cycles. The cross has also myths and rites of healing attached to it. It was believed to promote fertility of humans, animals, and crops as well as protect the home and its inhabitants from illness, hunger, and fire. They were often nailed to the beams inside the home or over the doorway entrance to the house. As the potato crop became the centerpiece of Irish agriculture, the cross was sometimes fixed to the roof beams with a wooden peg on which a potato was impaled, encouraging a rich harvest. A cross might be placed onto a basket of potatoes and taken to the fields at planting time to include Brigid's blessings on the crop. Frequently, the previous year's crosses were burned at Imbolc and their ashes were buried or scattered over the land. This is believed to be a direct link to rites of burning at Lughnasadh, where a portion of the harvest was re-dedicated to the Gods. In more recent years, the cross has been called simply "lucky" by many.

The St. Brigid's cross was often used to bless the Imbolc meal. Sometimes (as in the Threshold Rite in Chapter 6) the cross served as a placemat for the food. Crosses then took their places over doorways, mantles, or were nailed to the crossbeams of the house or stable to ensure a year of health and plentiful food.

St. Brigid save us from all fever, famine, and fire . . .

—An Imbolc Prayer

HOW TO MAKE A ST. BRIGID'S CROSS

To make your own St. Brigid's cross, you can gather rushes, but wheat stalks, grass, or other reeds will be suitable too. If you are using dry or brittle pieces, you may need to soak them in water to soften them. They can also be made from pipe cleaners or wires, which I have used below:

1. Take one piece and hold vertically, and fold another piece in half around the mid-point of the first.

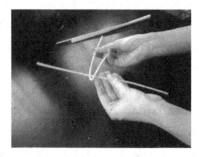

2. Take a third piece and fold around the second piece, parallel to the first. The pieces should now make a cross shape.

3. Take a fourth piece and fold around the third so that it is parallel with the first piece.

 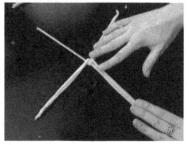

4. Continuing clockwise, repeat the process at each arm of the cross, until the cross reaches the size you would like. Keep the pieces tight and flat against one another, not overlapping, so that the center makes a definitive square. This is a good opportunity to meditate or pray, particularly on or for something you wish to bring into your life via Brigid.

5. When the center reaches the size you would like, tie the ends of the four spokes together as in the image below.

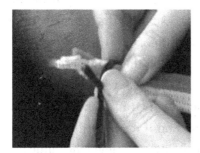 

6. Bless and hang in your home or give to a loved one!

A traditional blessing from some parts of Ireland when hanging a St. Brigid's cross says, *"May the blessing of God and the Trinity be on this cross, and on the home where it hangs and on everyone who looks at it."*

A Neo-Pagan version for Brigid may be said, *"May Brigid bless and keep this home. May the blessings ever grow. May all who cross my threshold know always the promise of spring. Blessed be this cross, Brigid! Blessed be my home!"*

IMBOLC DIVINATION

Divination was a favored pastime of Imbolc, possibly because the days were primarily spent around the fire keeping warm, passing time while the tides of Imbolc did their work on the land and the planting could truly begin. If you have a fireplace, replicating the hearth and ashes working could tell of the tides to come throughout the year. Smooth the ashes over the coals and check them in the morning. Do the ashes look like there might have been feet stepping on them? If so, Brigid has blessed you! If you do not have a fireplace, you can do what I do and leave a blanket and pillow by the radiator. Take a peek at the blanket the next morning and if it's been disturbed by something other than a pet; maybe it was Brigid who came by! If your ashes or blanket were not disturbed, it might be a telling of a tougher year to come. Make notes over the years of what you see and the events that followed.

As in the rites of old, leaving a Brigid ribbon out on Imbolc can still be an act of divination or a charm for healing. The piece can be actual ribbon or a strip of cloth, a sash, cord, or even a shawl as the lady in the story used. For best results, the piece should be long enough to wrap around the average person's head three times and tie into a knot. My coven cuts pieces of green, gold, or red cloth. On Imbolc eve, we light candles to Brigid and wave the cloth pieces over the flame nine times. I don't know if waving over the flames is part of the original rites, but it certainly sets the tone nicely in contemporary ones. Leave the cloth out by your window or, if you're able, on your front doorstep. Be sure to set out a nice cup of tea and a treat for Brigid as she passes by on Imbolc night. Measure the cloth before setting it and measure it again in the morning to see if it lengthened or decreased. A cloth that has seemingly lengthened indicates good luck to come. In this case, keep your Brigid ribbon for healing work. If you think your cloth has decreased in length, it may be time for meditation or reflection to be aware of any potential nasty luck ahead.

Traditionally, the ribbon is rubbed or drawn around the patient's afflicted area three times. Brigid's ribbons are best known for their effects on headaches, but also for toothaches, earaches, and sore throats. Members of my coven swear by them for alleviating anxiety or menstrual pain. When applying the ribbon, say the following invocation:

In the name of the Poet, the Smith, and the Healer,
Brigid make you whole again.

Knot the ribbon around the painful area. For best results, use the same ribbon each Imbolc, which will increase its potency.

Spell: Candle in the Doorway

(A similar version of this spell can be found in Chapter 10, for decision making.)

Take a paper plate and write or draw images of the following things:

Money

Health

Love

Trouble

If there are other things you hope to come to you in the next year, you may add those as well. You will want to give each item an equal section on the plate.

Set a red or yellow candle in the middle of the plate, and place the plate on a flameproof setting in a doorway. As the candle burns down, take note of where the wax spills. Lots of wax in that area indicates what you will have abundance of in the next year, for better or worse. Lack of wax indicates just that. Take a picture or save the plate and, at the following Imbolc, make note of how much came to manifest and how.

 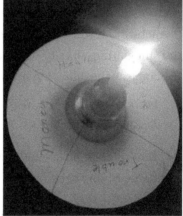

SUGGESTED RITES OF IMBOLC

As part of your Imbolc rite, you may want to include some sort of ritual cleansing—on yourself, your home, or both. This period of the year has traditionally involved some sort of cleaning, be it the fields for planting or a postpartum blessing on a new mother. The idea of spring cleaning may have its roots in Imbolc practices or others of a similar kind from different regions. Clearing and cleansing practices restored health and hygiene of the land, body, and home, but also symbolically restored a boundary between the forces of good and evil. The following rites are suggested for either one person or a group at Imbolc. Naturally, due to the actions involved in the second ritual, it is better recommended for a group but either can—and should— be augmented, enhanced, or changed to suit the needs of the practitioner(s).

An Imbolc Rite for One

Materials

Bowl of cleansing water (see Chapter 3 for suggested concoctions)

Three white candles

One yellow candle (do not use dripless candles)

A small food offering—preferably something sweet such as a cupcake or a cookie

Before beginning your Imbolc rite, reflect on recent events in your life: blessings, lessons, growth, and more. Create a space of comfort—perhaps with a cozy comforter and a cup of tea. (*As always, if you live in an environment where there is little or no privacy or quiet, don't be afraid to make use of your bathroom as sacred space.*) Focus on challenges that have come up in the space between Samhain and Imbolc, particularly any challenges you'd like to leave behind. Focus on what things you really wish to see come into your home, health, work, or self. Try, as best as you are able, to envision when throughout the months between the present Imbolc and the following Samhain that these things could happen (e.g., increased money after tax time, a new exercise routine when the weather warms, travel during the summer, a return to school in the fall).

Set your space for ritual with the four candles in holders, unlit, in a circle with the bowl of cleansing water in the middle. If you are in a region where snow is present, consider adding a lump of clean snow to your water just before beginning the rite. When the challenges and desired blessings are firmly in your mind, light the three white candles and let them burn for a while, but do not light the yellow one yet. Draw into your mind the vision of the Cailleach, the Winter Hag. Call upon her aloud or in your head:

Queen of Ice, Queen of Stone,
Hear me from your Frozen Throne,
Be here, be here, be here now!

As you chant or meditate on the words, envision her hair of snow, her skin of stone, and her eyes of ice, or however she appears to you. When you can see the image of the Winter Hag as firmly in your mind as you are able, cease the chant and begin to recount the challenges you've faced over the last few months either in your head or aloud. Next, tell her why you no longer want these things to hold you back. Then, listen. Listen to the words of the Winter Hag. Why were you faced with such challenges? Does she know? What words does she have for you?

When you are ready be released from these things, begin to chant or meditate the following:

Brigid has come! Brigid is welcome!
Brigid has come! Brigid is welcome!

Continue to chant until you can see or feel Brigid and her hair of sunbeams and long green cloak replace the space of the Winter

Hag. Light the yellow candle. Declare aloud or in your head what you want to be free from, such as, *"I release myself from stagnation in my career!" "I release the anger and pain at my ex!" "I release impatience with my children!"* Allow the dripping wax of the yellow candle to extinguish the flame of the white candles.

Sit with the burning yellow candle for a time, fixating on the image of Brigid in your mind. Tell her, aloud or in your head, what you wish to see blossom in your life over the spring, summer, and autumn. Then, as you did with the Cailleach, listen to any words that may come from Brigid, herself.

Finally, wash your face, the top of your head, and neck with the cleansing water. If you wear jewelry daily, wash that as well. If there are specific possessions that remind you of your troubles or troubling time, immerse them in water (if they are things that can be immersed—stones such as opal or selenite cannot be submerged) or simply flick some of the water over them if total submersion would damage them. Consider then changing your clothes as a symbol of putting on a new face, even if they are not new clothes. If you are able, burn the candle in a safe place in the center of your home—where you can see it, of course! No flames should be left unattended! The rite has concluded. Leave the sweet treat for the night on the windowsill. The sweet on the windowsill is a very old Imbolc tradition, one in which a sheaf of hay was also left for Brigid's cow, as Brigid was believed to travel the countryside with a bovine companion. Traditionally, it was expected that the poor or hungry would take the food during the night, keeping with the spirit of Brigid's aiding the poor. If this aspect speaks to you, consider taking an extra step in leaving the food where you do believe a hungry person will find it or simply drop off a food donation at a local pantry or soup kitchen.

Use the remaining water as a floor wash or sprinkle in the corners of your home to cleanse and renew your home.

After your rite, pamper yourself and relax for a bit. You'll want to be restored to meet all of the changes you wish to manifest!

An Imbolc Rite for a Group

Imbolc rites have involved community efforts for centuries. While some rites, such as the parading of the *Brídeog*, involved the entire community, many of the rites were private and focused on the family. In using this format, the following ritual can be performed with a group—be it a working magickal or spiritual group, friends, family, or a combination. Very young children might not fully understand the significance of the ritual, but could certainly be a part of it and enjoy the family time.

Materials

Cleansing water (purified or boiled water with a pinch of salt).

One large candle and a collection of tea light candles— one for each person in the group.

A bowl of earth or a decent-sized stone, perhaps one that needs a hefty fist or two hands to carry, but it doesn't need to be larger than that. This shouldn't be a gemstone or something decorative. It should come from a natural setting, such as a forest or field, or even a park.

A green or yellow cloth or shawl.

Cakes, cheese, or a potluck meal to share. Again, dairy products are most sacred to Brigid, but no matter the case, you'll want to be mindful of dietary restrictions and have appropriate options for your guests if they cannot consume dairy.

Set three stations on separate tables or in separate areas— one for the water, one for the candle, one for the stone. If need be, all three stations can be set atop a long table. If possible, the stations should be set with items reminiscent of Brigid or spring-time. Take liberties and be creative with how this is displayed.

One person should be selected to act as Brigid who will take the green or yellow cloth/shawl, and hide either outside or in the next room. This person can be of any gender. Some traditions had a young woman play this role; others had a man playing the role of "bringing Brigid" to the room. Choose the person you feel best embodies the energy of Brigid, regardless of their gender, and let them choose whether to "be" her or to "bring" her. When the Brigid player is ready, they will knock three times on the door or entryway to the room.

Group: *Who knocks there?*

Player: *It is I who touched the river and chased away the cold!*

Group: *Who is it who chased away the cold?*

Player: *It is I who chased the Winter Hag away!*

Group: *Who is it that chased the Winter Hag away?*

Player: *It is I who came with the wand, who breathed the breath back to the land! It is I! It is Brigid! It is I! It is Brigid!*

One Member of the Group: *Go on your knees, open your eyes, and let Brigid in!*

Remainder of the Group (some may choose to kneel): *She is welcome! She is welcome!*

The Player enters the room or house with the shawl or cloth on their head or in their arms and the group exclaims: *It is Life! It is Health!*

All hug, kiss, and welcome Brigid.

The Player walks to each station. At the stone, they tap it and say, *Winter Hag be gone and stay gone! You who have turned the land to ice, now you turn to stone! Spring has come throughout the land!*

Group: *Spring has come throughout the land!*

Player walks to water: *Water, you who have once been ice, now you thaw and warm again. Spring has come throughout the land!*

Group: *Spring has come throughout the land!*

Player walks to candle: *Child of the sun, perpetual flame! Come back to earth! It's spring again!*

Group: *Spring has come throughout the land!*

The following should either be read by the person embodying Brigid, or it can be split into sections and read by members of the group. (The poem for this rite was written by Nanci Moy.)

Cailleach

> *Winter Crone*
>
> *Shakes out her downy comforter*
>
> *Snow covers the land in sleepy silence*

Cailleach wanders

> *Tap taps her silvery rod*
>
> *Crystalline webs stretch across streams*
>
> *Stilling ripples, frosting breath*

Cailleach nears the sacred Well

> *Sighing, sips deeply*
>
> *Healing waters wash away the years*
>
> *Brigid flames forth*
>
> *Maiden melts Crone*

Brigid

> *Bright One*
>
> *Spreads her mantle wide*
>
> *Sees peeking snowdrops 'neath suckling lambs*

Brigid strides forward

> *Blesses brats girdles crosses dolls*
>
> *Drip drip the icicles on trees*
>
> *Into pools lakes streams rivers*

Brigid sings with the lark

> *Ripples with the waters*

Inspires all with crafty wisdom
Blesses hearth
Heart of home

Brigid is Come!
Brigid is Welcome!

Group members, individually, visit each station. At the Stone, they bid farewell to winter—to troubles or challenges of the previous season, or give thanksgiving for boons or blessings. At the Water station, they cleanse themselves—either washing faces or hands or flicking water around themselves as a way of cleansing the spiritual body that surrounds their physical one. At the Fire station, they place their hands around the flame as a way of allowing the sun's rays to nurture their new spring self.

While this is happening, chant or song is helpful to encourage the spirit of new spring. The albums *A Dream Whose Time Is Coming* produced by the Assembly of the Sacred Wheel, *Chants: Ritual Music from Reclaiming and Friends* by Serpentine Music Productions, or *La Lugh: Brighid's Kiss* by Gerry O'Connor and Eithne Ni Ullachaine have lovely selections to use for this portion of the rite. Websites can be found in the bibliography.

After each person has visited each station, it is time for food, divination if possible, or sharing of stories, experiences, or reflections. A small portion of the food should be set aside in honor of Brigid. The water can be sent home with guests in bottles so that all can use it in renewing their homes.

A Brigid Baby Blessing

I receive a lot of requests for baby blessings. They are sweet and fun. If you would like to perform a Brigid-inspired blessing for a baby, the following may prove helpful. My experience has taught me that short and simple but heartfelt rituals for children are the way to go.

Set the space with a candle, a small bowl of water, and a small bowl of soil. Parents and other guests, if attending, should chant *Brid is Come! Brid is Welcome!* several times to set the space.

Anoint the baby's forehead with drops of water on your fingertips, making a thrice-circular motion. Say the following: *May Brigid grant you Health.*

Wave the candle three times before the baby and say: *May Brigid bring you passion.*

Taking a wet finger, dip into the soil and leave a tiny mark of earth on the baby's forehead. Say: *May Brigid bring you the strength of the earth, and may you always have a solid path to walk on.*

Parents and any other guests attending may wish to impart their blessings on the baby at this point.

Conclude the rite by saying: *May Brigid bring you all these things and more, enough to fill the sea. May Brigid bless each step you take from the day you first begin to stand. Blessed be, Brigid! Blessed be Brigid upon you!*

CHAPTER 9

Brigid and Animals

"Brigid at Imbolc," by Carey A. Moore.

St. Bride's Charm

The charm put by Bride the beneficent,
On her goats, on her sheep, on her kine.
On her horses, on her chargers, on her herds,
Early and late going home, and from home.
To keep them from rocks and ridges,

From the heels and the horns of one another,

From the birds of the Red Rock,

And from the Luath of the Feinne,

From the blue peregrine hawk of Creag Duilion,

From the brindled eagle of Ben-Ard,

From the swift hawk of Tordun,

From the surly raven of Bard's Creag,

From the fox of the wiles,

From the wolf of the Mam,

From the foul-smelling fumart,

And from the restless great-hipped bear,

From ...

From ...

From every hoofed four feet,

And from every hatched of two wings.

—Traditional

Earth Goddesses typically have a penchant for working with animals. They speak their language, understand their impulses, and command their movements. As Earth Goddess, perhaps also in her Warrior Goddess guise, and certainly in her role as the Springtime Goddess, Brigid had a responsive relationship with animals.

In the practices of earth-based spiritualities and Goddess worship, there is a frequent element of animal symbolism. When working these paths, animals may appear in synchronistic moments, in dreams, or other images. Animal appearances are important, but the meaning of such appearances can be confusing. In the search for possible meanings, there is a strong tendency among magick communities and practitioners to associate all animal symbolism with the practices and beliefs of the indigenous peoples of the Americas. Quite commonly, Celtic animal symbolism is interchanged with perceived Native American animal symbolism. These assumptions are, more often than not, quite far from the truth. The beliefs of the different nations in the Americas vary and blanket symbolism does not apply. In addition, making the assumption that one facet of a Native American practice has an automatic parallel in Celtic spirituality is incorrect at best, disrespectful or tokenistic at worst.

Yet, this does not mean that practitioners of faiths other than those of the Native Americans should avoid inspiration from spirit animals. The father of a close friend of mine, himself a Native American, once explained that working with animal symbolism is a deeply personal experience, not one that can be quickly explained by books or websites. My own experience with animal symbolism has come with observing what is unique about a creature in the context of nature. For example, dragonflies undergo a massive transformation from nymph to maturity. They also haven't changed much over the course of millions of years of evolution. Somehow, dragonflies "got it right" the first time. When I see a dragonfly, I personally accept it as a sign that some positive development is on the way or that I'm doing what I should be doing. But my understanding of dragonfly symbolism will vary widely from that of someone else. Even my friend's father took the appearance of a dragonfly as a message from the Great Spirit, as that is what the creature meant to him. In working with Brigid Magick, it may prove helpful to understand a little more about the symbol of the animal in the context of Brigid lore. Again, your personal connections trump the definitions found in any book, but if you by chance happen to encounter a specific animal through dreams, visions, or in person, knowing more about Brigid's relationship to the animal will provide more fodder for thought. Animal encounters underscore important parts of the spiritual journey. Paying attention to these encounters and giving them due process of thought will enrich magickal work.

To the Celts, the appearance of wild animals contained omens, and frequently ominous ones. Birds were usually a negative sign. A sudden flock of birds from the coast could mean a storm was coming. Ravens and vultures meant death was near. The natural inclination of scavenger birds to appear at a place where death was present was a frightening sign for a people who depended on animal signs to alert them to danger. Even today, the appearance of a single magpie is considered a bad sign. A limerick about the magpie says, "One for sorrow, two for joy . . ." Magpies mate for life and seeing one alone may mean its partner met an untimely demise and is therefore a bad sign. While researching this book, a friend and I visited an ancient site that tragically had also been the site of a murder several months before. As we pulled up to the site, a single magpie sat still in middle of the road, staring right at us—a definitive symbol of the sorrow that had so recently taken place. Indeed, rotting flowers left by friends of the victim still littered the ground and the air was so heavy and eerie, we left before we found what we hoped to see.

In general, Brigid's relationship with animals was less ominous. Even birds were not the typical beacons of sorrow so far as Brigid was concerned. Larks and blackbirds would begin to sing around Imbolc, and their song meant life would shortly return to the wintry landscape. Brian Wright points out in *Brigid: Goddess, Druidess and Saint* that many of the animals associated with Brigid held a high status in the Celtic world and still do, as dairy products are a major part of Irish agriculture. Most of Brigid's animals were domesticated and essential to farmers, such as the cow whose milk products would sustain vital food sources during lean times. Because of her region of origin, the animals listed below are primarily found in the northern regions of the Northern Hemisphere. It would be interesting to hear about correlations practitioners from the Southern Hemisphere may find.

BEE

In Glastonbury, there is a place called Bride's Mound, a site where a monastery once stood and one where St. Brigid is believed to have visited. This place is also called Beckery, which is likely derived from *bheach na hAorai,* roughly meaning *Mound of Bees.* This was a pilgrimage site, a legendary first stop along the travel to the Tor. It highlights Brigid's relationship to the bee. Bees were considered by ancient Celts to be musical and productive creatures, reminiscent of Brigid's Bard spirit and even that of the Smith—the honey being the product of the bee's work in the same manner that iron is the product of the forge. To see bees may signify a gift of artistic inspiration from Brigid. It could also mean hard work shall shortly reap benefits. True to the pilgrimage spirit, the bee may also signify a new journey, either travel or of spirit.

BLACK ROOSTER

The black rooster is a symbol of Maman Brigitte. In many cultures, including Ireland, the rooster represents banishing negativity. The rooster's crow means dawn is imminent. Experiencing a black rooster in your work with Brigid may mean a time of danger or fear has passed. Because of its connection to Maman Brigitte, it may also be a sign to listen to advice of your ancestors, or serve as a reminder to pay them homage or pray for them.

BOAR

Once, in an area of woods to the north of Kildare, there lived a wild boar. This boar was brash and cruel and would never allow other pigs to approach it, keeping all acorns and apples to itself. Hungry and angry, the other pigs called for Brigid who came to their aid. With her staff, Brigid blessed the northern woods with

peace and the spirit of sharing, so that thereafter was harmony in
the woods. The wild boar became the leader of the pigs and cared
for them for all of his days.

—TRADITIONAL TALE

Boars had poignant significance to Celtic spiritual practices. Perhaps because of danger in hunting the animal, the boar was a symbol of bravery, battle, and warriorship. The great war and death Goddesses were often symbolized by the boar. In some stories, the boar was a shape-shifter and, therefore, representative of the Otherworld as well. Pork was a coveted dish among the Celts and a prime symbol of hospitality, with the meat frequently served at ritual feasts used to seal agreements. In this story, the angry boar and starving pigs are probably an analogy for a community of people, possibly one whom either the historical St. Brigid or another woman of renown helped negotiate some sort of truce among them. Brigid was even said to possess a boar herself, named Triath: the King of the Boars.

In Brigid Magick, the boar represents bravery, protection, and leadership, but also cooperation, kindness, and diplomacy.

COW

The infant Brigid was a sensitive child. Her Druid father worried
as whenever she nursed from her mother's breast, she threw up
what she consumed. No ordinary cow or sheep milk could sus-
tain her either, and she threw up all food that she ate. Still, her
appearance was one of health and she grew although she could
not eat. "I know what it is," said the Druid. "She cannot take from
a human or beast, for her powers are greater than mortal-kind. I
shall summon the red-eared cow from the Summerland and from
this beast shall she feast for all time." The cow came to the Druid,

its immortal milk sustaining the child. From that day forward,
they were together always, Brigid and her beloved cow. Whenever
she or anyone else were in need of food, this blessed cow would
always provide.

—TRADITIONAL TALE

Above all animals, the cow is the one most often associated with Brigid, particularly a white cow with red ears. The coloring of the cow is a symbol of the Otherworld. The cow's ability to provide milk, which supported hungry communities during lean months, was viewed as a miracle. Many divine animals in the Celtic canon, particularly bulls or cattle, were described as being white with red ears. In early Irish Christianity, children were even baptized with cow's milk. Images of cattle were used decoratively on Celtic objects and artwork, evoking strength, ferocity, and virility.

As milk production returned with the first light of Imbolc, Brigid's image of walking alongside the cow symbolizes the earth bringing food and health back into the world.

Other myths of Brigid's cow tell of a story of a milkless cow that could suddenly produce after Brigid tended to it, or a cow that could feed the hungry when there was no other food to be found. Brigid's mythical cow could heal the sick and could be milked three times more often than a mortal cow. If the situation called for it, Brigid herself could turn water into milk, a milk that could heal the toughest illness. But if the cow were mistreated or stolen by thieves, all of the elements of the land could not protect the culprit from the Goddess-Saint's vengeance. Brigid and her cow were nearly inseparable. One could consider the cow to be Brigid's personal spirit animal and closest companion. The Sacred Cow is believed by some scholars to have symbolized the sacredness of motherhood. Through her milk, the life-force itself was sustained and nourished. By no means a passive giver of milk, Brigid represents an active mother fighting for the health, safety, and well-being of her offspring.

To encounter or dream of a cow when working with Brigid is a signal of divine communion with this Goddess, receiving her blessings and becoming in touch with her work in the physical world. The cow may also represent healing, messages from the spirit world, and entry into a new chapter of life.

DOG

A sad and wretched hound came to the house of Brigid one day, begging for food. Moved by the dog's mange and bony body, Brigid gave him one-fifth of the bacon she was preparing for the people in the house. The dog swallowed the meat in one gulp and begged for more. As she could not bear to see the animal so hungry, Brigid gave him yet another piece of bacon, leaving only three-fifths left for the household. A house guest, whom Brigid thought was asleep, had spied on her and saw what bacon was left. Surely, there would not be enough to feed the inhabitants and so the guest told Dubthach, Brigid's father, of the canine being fed what was needed for the house. Dubthach, angry, rushed to Brigid and demanded the truth. Brigid admitted to having fed the dog from the household goods, but then said to her father of the bacon pieces, "Count them." Dubthach counted the pieces in the pan and sure enough, there was plenty for the house—more than had been in the stores before they'd gone to bed the night before. The household ate plentiful food, with the exception of the tattling guest. Brigid took the guest's portion down the road to feed the poor, her new dog friend trotting along beside her.

—INSPIRED BY TRADITIONAL TALE

The dog, or hound, in Celtic mythology was significant as a hunting or battlefield companion. Brigid's encounter with the dog in this story is more about kindness and compassion than battle, but perhaps it suggests a battle against poverty. Pork, as discussed above, was a great symbol of hospitality and the guest's unwillingness to take part in Brigid's hospitality to a suffering creature is a symbol of selfishness. Contemporary dogs depend greatly on humans and a dog, like the one above, that does not have a human to care for it is likely to die. Brigid's care for the dog is a reminder that giving of ourselves does not always require sacrifice of all that we have, but only a portion of it. It is also a reminder that there is more than enough for all in this world, and sharing does not always create want.

If dog or hound appears in your dreams or life while working with Brigid, it may warrant reflection on what resources you have in plenty and what things you might be able to share. Resources do not necessarily equal money. They certainly don't have to mean bacon. Resources might include listening to someone who needs an ear or helping a neighbor who needs a hand with a project. Dog and hound ask us to look at where needs are present and encourage us to figure out ways to help.

DUCK

One day, Brigid walked along the road and passed a pond where she saw a flock of ducks swimming in the water, and sometimes flying through the air, following their natural instincts. Drawing on her own instincts, Brigid summoned them to come to her. The ducks took to the air and began to fly to her in unison, without fear or hostility, as though her own calls were synonymous with theirs. Brigid touched them with her hand and took them into her arms and then let them go flying back into the air and to the pond. From this motion, it could be understood that all the beasts and birds of nature were subject to Brigid, beloved by her, and she beloved by them.

—Traditional Tale

Brigid's ability to summon the wild ducks is a trait of hers as Earth Goddess. She quickly attuned with the ducks' natural tendencies and was able to change their direction at will. In your work, the appearance of ducks may mean becoming deeper in touch with your own natural instincts. It may also mean contributing order and leadership, perhaps in a situation slightly foreign to you. Although Brigid was not a duck, she was able to direct the flock. Seeing or dreaming of a duck—particularly a flock of ducks—may mean a similar sort of responsibility is required of you.

DRAGON

St. Brendan came to visit Brigid to share a strange encounter with sea dragons on his most recent voyage. He had been standing on a rock and saw below him two dragons attempting to drown one another. Suddenly, one cried out in a human voice, "I beseech you in the name of St. Brigid! Let me be!" The other dragon withdrew at once and swam to the depths of the sea. St. Brendan wondered why the dragon had referred to Brigid, despite the fact that he himself was present. Puzzled herself, Brigid suggested they each make a statement of their beliefs. St. Brendan said, "I declare I have never crossed seven waves without turning my mind to God!" Brigid then said, "I confess that since I first fixed my mind upon God, I have never taken it off and never will until the end of time." Sensing Brendan's continued confusion, Brigid explained that because he was a voyager of the sea and therefore constantly exposing himself to danger, it was natural that he concentrate on his safety rather than God at all times. She herself lived with less danger and could devote more time to her God. He certainly had not forgotten his faith as he praised his God after every seventh wave. Brendan found consolation in the explanation.

—TRADITIONAL TALE

St. Brendan, who was also referred to as "The Navigator," was supposedly a contemporary of the historical St. Brigid, and is believed to have originally told this story himself. While St. Brendan probably did not come across a physical dragon, the term might be used to describe a weathered seaman or even a pirate of sorts. (Then again, who knows? Maybe he did come across a real dragon!) Another version has St. Brendan witnessing this same exchange between two whales—the description of dragon may simply be a label for a great sea creature. He may have marveled at how far St. Brigid's renown had taken her and maybe felt inferior that other seafarers would call upon her before himself. Brigid's kindness and compassion was able to comfort Brendan, without denigrating her own self.

If you see a dragon in dreams or meditations while working with Brigid, it may mean that your sphere of influence has extended further than you might imagine. It might also be a call to set ego aside and perhaps show compassion for a competitor. It also might be a sign to call for Brigid's help if facing something threatening.

If you see a dragon in real life, email me immediately and let me know where so that I can plan a visit!

FOX

One day, a peasant man walked through the woods just beyond his King's palace and saw a fox, mistaking it for a wild animal. In reality, the fox was a trained pet of the King that had learned various tricks and entertained the court, daily. But the man did not know this, and in need of fur for the upcoming winter, killed the fox and took its pelt home. Members of the court saw him doing the deed and reported it to the King's guard, who sought out the man, put him in shackles, and brought him before the King.

The furious King ordered the man's execution and his wife and children be sold as slaves, unless the man give him a fox that could perform all of the tricks the previous fox had done. Until that time came, the man would stay in prison and his possessions be seized. When Brigid learned of the situation, she was furious at the injustice. She ordered her horses be harnessed and rode her chariot, fast as the wind, to the King's palace. As she traveled, a wild fox ran up to her chariot and jumped aboard. It nestled under her cloak and hid as she entered the palace and entreated the King, arguing for the man's innocence, citing that it was an accident and begging the King's pardon.

The angry King refused to listen and reiterated that the man would not be released until the King received a fox as tame and clever as the one he lost. It was then that Brigid released the wild fox from beneath her cloak. Before the eyes of the King and his court, she summoned the fox to do the cleverest of tricks—far more clever than that of the King's pet. The King was delighted with the new fox. He ordered the man be unshackled and let him go with a bonus of wealth to bring home to his family.

After he and Brigid had left, the wild little fox slipped away from the palace and despite all of the horses, hounds, and men sent after him, the fox returned to his den and was never recaptured. Brigid was once again praised for her championship of an innocent man and the summoning of a wild fox.

—TRADITIONAL TALE

Foxes typically have a presence in many cultures as a cunning, tricky creature. Indeed, the fox can adapt and adjust to many a difficult situation. I have heard claims that the modern fox is rapidly evolving in areas where fox hunting is common to be smaller, sleeker, and quicker to better escape hunting hounds. In this story, the fox is not only a cunning creature, but assists Brigid in her desire to bring justice where it is due.

Should a fox cross your path or enter your thoughts and dreams, reflect on this story. Where do you see injustice occurring? How might your voice lend assistance? Unconventional, or daresay "tricky" methods may be in order. If you are running up against something much bigger than yourself, the appearance or a dream of a fox may mean that Brigid wants to help you win your battle.

HORSE

While Brigid be locked away, cold in Ben Nevis, a prisoner of the Winter Hag, she will not wait forever. She need not wait long. Come Imbolc eve, Oenghus shall ride on the White Horse of Spring, out of the Otherworld to carry her away while the Hag turns back to stone.

—TRADITIONAL TALE

The horse was certainly one of the more revered animals in the Celtic world. For transportation, battle assistance, hunting, and even food when times were really rough, the horse was an essential part of existence. To have a horse meant accomplishment or victory was evident. To have your horse attacked, or to attack one belonging to someone else, would render your endeavors or theirs ineffective. Brigid's attack on the horses of the soldiers who refused to assist her sisters underscores the importance of the horse. In the myth above, Brigid also had horses that came to her own aid.

Brigid's relationship to the horse is all about movement and triumph, particularly if the horse is white. White bulls, cows, and horses were believed to be direct emissaries from the Otherworld and, in the case of Brigid, brought liberation. Encountering a horse on your Brigid journey may mean a personal sort of liberation, or success over a daunting task.

OX

Wealthy friends of Brigid paid her a visit one day, bringing with them offerings for her work with the poor. In their eagerness to help Brigid's work, they left their house without caretakers. While they were gone, robbers took oxen from the premises and led them to the river. They removed their clothes and hung them on the oxen's horns so they would not get wet as they crossed the water. The oxen turned and ran, the garments still on their horns, to the place where Brigid resided, leaving the robbers bare, cold, and embarrassed on the banks of the river.

—Inspired by traditional tale

In the *Lebor Gabála Érenn* (*The Book of the Taking of Ireland*) Brigid is described as having two royal oxen named Fe and Menn. In being described as royal, they, like many of Brigid's animals, were chiefly meant as "the best." Oxen are known for being loyal and supportive animals. They certainly played an extensive role in the development of agriculture due to their strength and ability to carry great loads enormous distances. To the Celts, they also represented power and fertility and were an honored sacrifice in the most important rites.

This terribly funny story of the oxen helping punish thieves not only illustrates their loyalty to Brigid and their masters, but also underscores Brigid's work for justice.

Experience with the ox denotes great strength and determination, as well as making the choice to do what's right for all. Like the oxen in the story, it may mean quietly going along with something you don't agree with until the opportunity to divert your energy to something else arises. In addition, ox knows its limits and will stop in its tracks when it has been pushed far enough. In that, encountering ox is also about recognizing boundaries.

SALMON

In the story of Boann, the Salmon of Knowledge knew the mysteries of the world, and kept it for themselves. When Boann released its waters, the salmon wandered, looking for the magickal hazelnuts that once fed them all the knowledge in existence. They may have lost their source, but the world gained from their loss and indeed, Brigid was born from it.

To experience salmon on your journey with Brigid may be a sign of innate wisdom and divine inspiration. If you experience a loss and then encounter salmon, it is a reminder that not all is lost and there are benefits to be gained from the experience.

SHEEP

Brigid was once tending sheep, and a robber came along and took seven of her flock. Brigid saw the robber and said nothing, watching him hurry into the hills, along with her seven. She whispered a prayer to the sheep and the land and she knew her flock would be complete when the sun set that evening. Indeed it was so. Her seven returned without injury and when the robber crossed the greatest hill, turned around to find none.

—TRADITIONAL TALE

As the springtime Goddess, the penultimate sign of Imbolc's first days was the lactation of the sheep along with the cattle. Brigid also owned the king of the rams, a beast named Cirb, who could be encountered when seeking Brigid for wisdom while she is tending her own flock of sheep. Like cattle, sheep were a staple of the Celtic food source and economy. The idea of Brigid as the Shepherdess is a sign of caretaking for community, and of a gentle kind of leadership. She puts her faith that all will be well, even when her own sheep are stolen.

The appearance of sheep in your Brigid journey may speak of health and renewal, like the early tides of Imbolc, caring for others, or some sort of leadership role. Moreover, it calls upon a sort of faith that all will be well even when things seem daunting and dangerous—like having faith the early days of spring will chase away the pain of the late winter days.

SNAKE

The serpent will come from the hole
On the brown Day of Bride,
Though there should be three feet of snow
On the flat surface of the ground.

—A Scottish hymn sung at Imbolc

One of my favorite effigies of Brigid shows her clutching a snake. Some believe this is inherited from Roman iconography, but many older poems to Brigid (like the one above) reveal her relationship with the snake to be more about the beginnings of springtime. The myth of driving the snakes out of Ireland has been part of St. Patrick's canon of miracles for quite some time, although snakes have never been part of the Irish animal kingdom due to the fact that the soil of Ireland is not conducive for their burrowing. Snakes do live in Scotland and England, however, and their appearance from the ground in early February is one of the first signs of spring, like the lactation of the ewes.

In Brigid Magick, the symbol of the snake is one of reawakening and rebirth. Snakes are admired for their ability to grow a new skin and shed the old one. The practices of cleansing and renewal at Imbolc mirror this very process. Should you experience a snake on your Brigid journey, know that what might have been dormant in you or your life for a time is bound to receive new energy and renewal. Breathe, be present in it, and embrace the change.

VULTURE

Nearly all of Brigid's associations are with birth and life. Few of her symbols denote death, but the vulture may be one of them. While I could not find any poems or stories linking Brigid to the scavenger bird, some passages I did find linked Brigantia in England with the vulture. Not surprisingly, scavenger birds such as the vulture, raven, or crow were linked with warrior Goddesses, as these creatures were likely to be found around places of battle, feasting on the remains of the dead. Vultures can be found wherever death is present, be this from a war, a hunt, or the natural passing of a forest creature. Dead bodies of humans or animals are harbingers of bacteria and disease. Naturally, a battlefield strewn with the dead would be a serious problem for a community, particularly if the dead lay near a water source that could be contaminated by bacteria from decomposition. While seemingly morbid, vultures would eliminate much of the danger from these environments and in what may seem a form of nature's irony, creatures of death could help secure future community health.

Should you come across a vulture, something is likely to have met its end. Some examples might be a move, a job change, or the end of a relationship. In some cases, it may indicate a physical death of a loved one. No matter what the case may be, let it be a reminder that Brigid's vulture brings health through an ending. Acknowledge the pain, bless it, and release it when you are ready. Like snake, vulture also marks a new beginning.

EXERCISE: TO FIND YOUR BRIGID ANIMAL

If your mind were a tunnel, what might it look like? Take quiet space and time, and with closed eyes examine the inside of your mind as though it were a tunnel traveling downward. Begin to explore this tunnel and follow it. Deeper and deeper, you explore this personal pathway. Keep going.

On your own time, allow this tunnel to open into a pasture—one that overlooks a river. The pasture is crowded with sheep, cows, and other animals. Observe them for a moment. Then, turn to your right, where you will see Brigid standing with her shepherd's staff and her white cow with red ears. Brigid will ask you a question. Answer honestly. She will then beckon for you to follow her and the cow. They lead you around the pasture to a cave.

Enter the cave. Do not be afraid of the depths or the size. You cannot be harmed. Go inside and journey deeper and deeper until you reach a place where the cave stops.

It is silent, except for the lowing of Brigid's cow at the mouth of the cave, seemingly summoning something in the dark.

You start to become aware of a presence beside you. You may hear rustling or cloven hooves. The animal brushes against you. You may feel fur or scales or something else altogether. You start to make out the shape of glowing eyes and, in time, your eyes adjust enough to the dark so that the full shape of the animal appears. This is your Brigid Spirit animal. Sit with the animal and communicate with it, or simply be present with it. It may ask you to follow it to another location. Do what feels right.

When your time is done, give thanks to the animal, to Brigid, and her sacred white cow. Journey back up the tunnel, as in the way that you came until you are back in the present. Record thoughts or visions.

CHAPTER 10

Brigid Magick

Earth Goddess, Well Spirit, Forge Patron, Bard, and Druidess . . . above all, Brigid meant magick. Each of her areas of patronage were believed to be endowed with magick as their very existence (clean water, the forge's transformative abilities, creative inspiration, and more) was seen as otherworldly. Brigid's magickal career did not end when the old Celtic world became Christianized. St. Brigid's stories are packed with spell castings, encounters with wizards, and even curses. In fact, a number of spells in this chapter are derived from St. Brigid's magickal lore.

But what *is* magick? In an age of incredible scientific progress, is there still a place for magick? Most of what our ancestors deemed magickal is now explained by science, yet many still believe in magick and are drawn to it. The word, spelled with a "k" to differentiate it from stage-performance or parlor-trick type of magic, has many incarnations. For some, magick describes the sense of heightened joy when perfect synchronistic events line up to make a particular moment feel extraordinary. It also describes a strangely kinetic connection between people otherwise unfamiliar to one another. Finally, magick refers to the energetic and spiritual practice of manifesting change. Magick doesn't attempt to negate science. It explores, as it always has, the areas science has yet to label and embraces the soul beneath the matter.

Brigid's magick is known for manifesting quickly, but also for manifesting in surprising ways. True to one of her images of having two faces, one beautiful and one harsh, Brigid Magick can unfold in a similar fashion: gracious blessings often combined with rough lessons. One famous trademark of Brigid spells is their delivery of exactly what you've asked for just in time to show you that you don't actually need it, but also revealing other options even more rewarding. Brigid magick is accessible. It is frequently beloved by healers, justice workers, parents, and artists, but is not confined to that list. Wherever there is a need for innovation, strength, or healing, there is fodder for Brigid Magick.

I have seen contemporary ceremonialists invoke Brigid in elaborate rituals; I have also seen her drawn into ecstatic, spontaneous rites. I have experienced success in both formats and more. Yet matters of home are so very entrenched in the history and identity of Brigid that many of her rites can be performed with simple tools found about the house. Often, work within the house is tantamount to what tools are used.

KNOWING BRIGID

Working with a Deity is effective when the relationship is made before requests are petitioned or spells cast. Like a relationship with a person, a bond and trust must be made before asking for great favors. Naturally, many would sweep in to help a stranger in an emergency, but we probably can't call up a stranger and expect them to help us move or pick up our cat from the vet. Likewise, it is best to get to know Brigid before asking for her help. While her nature is one of helping those in need without question, swifter and more quality assistance will come with familiarity.

Take time to get to know Brigid the way you would a new friend. Create a space for her in your home, if you can. (Suggested methods are listed in the next section.) Leave out a cup of tea or a treat periodically, or light a candle next to her effigy just to say hello. Regular observance of Imbolc rites, as you would regularly observe a friend's birthday, will help solidify you to the natural cycle of a Brigid year. Forge the relationship before you use it. She is the Smith after all, and would respect your forging!

USING BRIGID MAGICK

Brigid practitioners often dedicate space in their home to work with her. These spaces are ideally set up near the fireplace or radiator, but are fine anywhere the pulse or the sense of "hominess" is strongest. Fireplaces speak to our ancestral memories as the center of the home. Kitchens and living rooms are good options for Brigid working space as both spaces hold the pulse of the modern home. Finding the best place for your Brigid work takes time. The pulse of your specific home may not be in the kitchen or at a fireplace. Listen and feel where the strongest sense of "home" is felt when you walk about the place. My partner and I do not have a fireplace, but we are fortunate to have a spare room where our altars reside. This is a nice respite from our crazy NYC lives, but we've also worked Brigid magick in the living room, which is the first place guests walk into and is the nerve center of our home. But for years, I kept a Brigid altar crammed next to the radiator in my old, tiny bedroom as that was the place I felt the most at peace after a long day.

Ideally, one would construct an altar to Brigid and tend it regularly. Altars can be simple. A small table or a bookshelf is sufficient. Most Brigid altars I have seen include a candle to represent the Forge, a vessel of water to represent the Well, and usually something green to represent the Earth. My Brigid altar is crowded with effigies I've collected of Brigid over the years, trinkets from Ireland and New Orleans, poems friends have written to her, and tiny St. Brigid's crosses I've received. It's not organized or tidy, but it reflects my experiences and relationship with her. One Brigid devotee I know keeps an impeccably neat altar on a beautiful table in her living room, only containing a Brigid statue and a candle closed in a glass box, which she keeps perpetually lit. Another has populated her altar with figurines of sheep and cows, as well as photos of herself and her husband as they both love Brigid and used a Brigid blessing at their wedding. Although these altars are all different, the Brigid energy is palpable all the same on each. If keeping an altar is not possible, devising a simple routine when approaching your sacred space will have the same effect. The ritual and routine will allow the desired manifestation to take place.

In my community, many people, particularly young people, struggle to find privacy in small, crowded apartments. Many cannot dedicate permanent sacred space to Brigid. Some wrap up items that evoke the sense of Brigid Magick (examples to follow), and pull them out when ready to work. Others privately designate a quiet area of a park for their work. These solutions are perfectly appropriate and appeal to Brigid's creative, innovative energy.

The following spells and practices are, for the most part, guidelines. You may find inspiration to do them differently and, seeing as Brigid is a Goddess of inspiration and innovation, it would be foolish not to follow your instincts! A very few require more specific follow-through, either because of the way the spell is written or because of traditional practices that have fed the practice.

My Brigid Altar. On it, I keep a flame originally lit at the Perpetual Flame at Kildare, a bowl of water (Brigid well water, if I have it on hand, and sometimes a little perfume for scent and loveliness), a little anvil, various St. Brigid's crosses, a prayer card from St. Brigid's Church on the Lower East Side, a Maman Brigitte doll I made, a "Brigid the Protector" action figure, and sundry trinkets from Brigid rituals I've attended, plus an iron nail I forged myself at a blacksmith shop. It reflects my journey with Brigid. Yours should reflect your own journey.

CASTING SACRED SPACE FOR BRIGID MAGICK

Casting a circle is a common practice among magick practitioners to hold the energy in place and create sacred space. To cast the circle, you must imagine and envision as where thoughts go, energy flows. For each of the following incantations, you must focus and envision them as much as possible while you speak them. The more focus and dedication you give your casting, the stronger and more potent your magick will be. The following is a suggested casting for a Circle for Brigid Magick:

> Stand facing the East and say the following: *"I summon the powers of East—Brigid's bright powers of Dawn! As you bring light to the Spring, bring light to my work. Hail and Welcome!"*
>
> Turn to the South: *"I summon the Powers of South—the Blazing Fires of Brigid's Forge! Shed all that does not aid my work! Fortify my work! Let it change the World! Hail and Welcome!"*
>
> Turn to the West: *"I summon the Powers of West—the Healing Powers of the Well! May my work flow and grow! May it stir and summon the depths of possibilities! Hail and Welcome!"*
>
> Turn to the North: *"I summon the Powers of North—the Strength of the Cold Mountains! Freeze all adversities! Solidify my Desires with the Weight of the Frozen Rock! Hail and Welcome!"*
>
> Reach to the sky: *"By the Powers of the Fiery Arrows!"*
>
> Reach to the ground: *"By the Powers of the Green Earth!"*
>
> Extend arms to your sides: *"I summon Brig, the Exalted One! Hail and Welcome! Hail and Welcome! Hail and Welcome!"*
>
> Your circle will then be cast.

The casting above is situated for practitioners in the Northern Hemisphere. If you are in the Southern Hemisphere, you may wish to substitute Fire for North and Ice for the South and cast the circle counter-clockwise, beginning in the East, and then casting North, West, and then South. In the Northern Hemisphere, energy is banished via counter-clockwise movement, as seen in the final seconds of whirlpools going down the drain. Therefore, casting a circle in the Northern Hemisphere is most effective when cast clockwise. Likewise, the movements in the Southern Hemisphere are opposite.

To release your circle when your work is done:

Turn to the North: *"Farewell to the Powers of North—as you came in peace, go in peace as well, but leave strength in my work. Keep my adversaries in your icy grasp. Hail and Farewell!"*

Turn to the West: *"Farewell to the Powers of West—as you came in peace, go in peace as well, but leave your misty whispers on my work. Wash away the obstacles to my manifestation. Hail and Farewell!"*

Turn to the South: *"Farewell to the Powers of South—as you came in peace, go in peace as well, but leave your sparks of manifestation. Allow the embers of my work to grow. Hail and Farewell!"*

Stand facing the East and say the following: *"Farewell to the powers of East—as you came in peace, go in peace as well! Though the day passes, the work of the sun remains. Remain also with my work. Hail and Farewell!"*

Reach to the sky: *"By the Grace of the Fiery Arrows!"*

Reach to the ground: *"By the Nurture of the Green Earth!"*

Extend arms to your sides: *"Hail Brig, the Exalted One! With thanks for your gifts, blessings, and attentions! Go if you must, stay if you will! My/Our circle is now released, but always and for eternity, Hail! Hail! Hail!"*

Your circle is open and rite ended.

INGREDIENTS FOR BRIGID MAGICK

Below are a couple of lists of ingredients commonly used in Brigid spells, which can also be used to charge Brigid space.

Plants: Dandelion, torranan, bay laurel, betony, watercress, wild carrot, the snowdrop, oak, white roses, lavender, cinnamon, or cassia.

Stones: Sunstone, ruby, emerald, moonstone, smoky quartz, garnet.

Other Items: Dairy products, tea, whiskey, beer, candles, clean water.

Common Brigid Magick Colors: Red, green, orange, yellow, white, purple.

SEASONS FOR DOING BRIGID MAGICK

While performing Brigid Magick will take on a daily devotional aspect and won't be tied to any one specific time of year, Brigid practitioners may discover that some times of the year will be better suited for certain aspects of Brigid Magick than others.

November, December, and January in the Northern Hemisphere or May, June, and July in the Southern Hemisphere. The Celtic calendar historically called these months "the dead months" or "the dead quarter," although specific terms and timing were and still are subjective by region. Being that this was the time when the Cailleach locked Brigid away, this is a good time for doing personal work and healing with Brigid.

Imbolc: January 31/February 1 in the Northern Hemisphere or July 31/August 1 in the Southern Hemisphere. Imbolc is a time for calling on Brigid for divination and for making healing amulets. Imbolc is also a time of house blessing and doing work on behalf of one's family or animals.

Springtime Magick. As Brigid is synonymous with springtime, the season is perfect for home blessings and cleansings. The natural push of spring means this is a good time for doing justice-oriented work. Magick practitioners of all traditions often use spring as a starting place, casting spells for things they wish to manifest later in the year, akin to planting crops or flowers.

Samhain: October 31/November 1 in the Northern Hemisphere or April 30/May 1 in the Southern Hemisphere. This is the holiday when the Cailleach whisked Brigid away for imprisonment in Ben Nevis, and the feast day of Maman Brigitte known as *Fet Gede*. This is a time for magick used for halting. If there is a habit or sequence of events that needs to slow down or stop altogether, this is a good time for casting such spells. This is a time when Brigid can help practitioners connect with their ancestors. It is also traditionally a powerful time of divination.

TIME OF DAY

Brigid was born at sunrise. The house in which she came into the world blazed into a flame that reached the sky and a pillar of fire rose from her head. Her very living breath gave new life to the dead.
—TRADITIONAL

Brigid Magick is excellent first thing in the morning. As mentioned above, she was born at sunrise, which may be a connection to her roots as a Goddess of springtime, her birth marking the return of growth and abundance. Evenings are often full of home and life obligations for many—preparing meals, caring for children or animals, wrapping up work. Mornings can be a time of quiet before the work of the day begins. If dawn is just an unfathomable time for you to make magick, set your sacred space with items for your intention the night before. The energies of dawn will still infuse the work when the sun rises. Even if mornings are difficult, I do encourage anyone who works with Brigid Magick to work with dawn energies periodically, even if not on a regular basis. If treated as a pilgrimage of its own, the early rising—painful as it might be—will reap great rewards as pilgrimages do.

These spells and rituals were compiled through research and practice. Even so, they are meant to be a guideline for the work. Brigid, being both a creative and practical Goddess, allows and encourages taking liberties to suit one's needs and inspirations.

A BASIC BRIGID OIL

The following oil is one I made with a friend early in my Brigid journey. Its recipe is a combination of essential oils known for their strength in magick potions, along with things specific to Brigid. I have seen and heard much success with this oil.

Materials

2 parts ylang ylang essential oil, 3 parts sandalwood essential oil, 5 parts rosewood essential oil, 3 parts sage essential oil, 2 parts chamomile essential oil.

Crushed dragon's blood resin.

1 small garnet or quartz crystal.

Dried flowers sacred to Brigid or essential oils of these plants—ones that are pleasing to your liking.

Sweet almond or mineral oil for the base. You can use olive oil in a pinch, but the scent isn't as enticing when you're not cooking with it!

Mix the oil at dawn near the pulse of your home. Another option: Mix this on the evening of Imbolc and leave it with your Brigid offerings throughout the night and dawn. For the strongest effect, prepare this oil at dawn, the day before Imbolc, and leave it for Brigid through the night and into the dawn of Imbolc itself. This will increase its potency several times over.

This oil can then be used for any Brigid Magick. Tiny portions of it may be augmented for specific spells. A drop of patchouli added to the mix will make a delightful Brigid prosperity spell. Mixing in a little extra rosewood oil along with some honey is a powerful shot to a romance spell. I have had success in adding pinches of cinnamon to Brigid creativity spells. If your skin is not sensitive to the ingredients, anointing yourself with the oil can attract the very things you seek. The Brigid oil alone can be used to better be in tune with the Goddess. This oil can anoint St. Brigid's crosses, candles, divinatory tools such as mirrors or tarot, or other ritual tools such as wands or athames (knives consecrated for use in magick ritual) that you plan to use for Brigid Magick.

Making an oil is its own spiritual process. It's not enough to simply mix the concoction together and wait for magick to happen. In making your basic Brigid oil, envision the things you want the oil to do. If you are tightly acquainted with Brigid, you might reflect on your experiences with her. If you are not familiar with

Brigid, embrace your curiosities. Meditate on what it is you *want* to know about Brigid. Take note of images, thoughts, words, or even colors that come to your mind as you mix. They may reveal important synchronicities later, clueing you in to more knowledge about Brigid.

Another tool to aid your oil making is the use of chant. Chanting a phrase describing what you'd like your oil to do strengthens it. Magick is energy and the energy of your vocal cords, breath, and rhythmic words will infuse the oil. The chant can be simple. The base oil might simply need a repeated chant of "Know Brigid, Know Brigid," or "Brigid Money, Brigid Money" for a prosperity spell, "Brigid Love, Brigid Love" for romance, and so forth. Simplicity is key in chant. Its wording should directly describe the desired outcome, but be simple enough so that the caster doesn't have to focus thoughts on the wording, and can focus more on the intention.

This recipe for Brigid oil is a good one to have on hand to anoint any Brigid spell, including those listed below.

A DEDICATION TO BRIGID

Brigid loves devotees and doesn't discriminate. Simply constructing a space to do your Brigid work will form the basis of a magickal relationship with her, but if you'd like to create a more formal relationship, lighting a candle before a Brigid effigy, such as a statue or a picture printed from the Internet, and announcing your desire to work with her will do the trick. However, if you'd like to perform a more formal ritual, the one below is a simple but powerful suggestion.

Materials

A large bowl—preferably glass

A votive or tea light candle—white, yellow, or orange

A water glass

An apple sliced into three parts—either top to bottom or across

Oak leaves and/or acorns

A combination of sacred Brigid flowers of your choosing

Set the votive candle in the water glass. You may need some pebbles or other tiny weights to weigh the bottom of the glass.

Set the glass and candle in the bowl and light the candle. Then, fill the bowl with water until the waterline is above the flame. Add the oak leaves, acorns, and flowers to the water, along with the cut apple.

Sit with the presence of the combination of the well and the flame of the forge. The rite can be performed at any time of day or season, but for greatest power, perform the ritual at dawn on Imbolc. This would be a good time to dedicate any jewelry, such as a St. Brigid's cross, or to consecrate the altar itself, which can be done with a sprinkling of water from the well.

Cast the circle with the suggested formula earlier in the chapter, under "Casting Sacred Space for Brigid Magick."

The rite will end when you feel an energy shift: a sense of peace, a burst of excitement, or the relaxation akin to a warm bath. Release the circle as recommended earlier in the chapter. Discard the water in a garden or park, declaring your dedication to Brigid complete and true. This rite may have profound moments, but some may find it quiet and uneventful. If you experience the latter, take heart in knowing that the shifts are yet to come.

BRIGID HEALING SPELLS

In performing magick, it is important to remember that a spell can complement medical treatment, but it should never replace the work and advice of a doctor.

Brigid's Ribbon

Lightly wrap a ribbon around the patient's head, neck, or other area three times (or rub the patient's afflicted area with the ribbon if working on an area other than the head), saying each time the invocation:

> *May the bright Forge burn,*
> *May the deep Well soothe,*
> *May the Green Earth reclaim,*
> *Blessed Brigid take away the pain.*

Knot the ribbon around the base of the head or afflicted area and let the recipient rest until the pain subsides.

This ribbon can be used for ailments throughout the year. You can also "recharge" the piece at the next Imbolc, increasing its potency.

I have seen this charm work first-hand on headaches. I have also seen it have a healing effect on menstrual pain.

A Healing Spell for Another Person

The following spell comes from a folktale called *Charm of the Sprain* in which Brigid healed a horse who broke a leg. This is particularly good for individuals recovering from accidents or surgeries. Be sure to get permission before performing the spell. Some individuals may not want to have magick practiced on them and permission from the recipient aids the strength of the spell.

Set a picture of the recipient or an object that belongs to them in your sacred space. Light three orange candles, anointed with the Brigid oil if you have it. After casting the circle, arrange the candles around the patient's photo or belongings and recite the following:

> *Bone to bone,*
> *Flesh to flesh,*
> *Sinew to sinew,*
> *And vein to vein,*
> *As Brigid healed that,*
> *May I heal this.*

Repeat the chant over and over until the words blur in your head. Keep the photograph or possession on the altar and light the candles surrounding it nightly until the person is healed. Keep candles lit only when you or someone else is at home. Do not leave candles burning unattended—it's not particularly beneficial to the spell and it is very dangerous. Repeat the incantation a few more times when relighting the candles each night. When the healing is complete, return the possession to the patient or remove the photo from your sacred space. Photos can either be returned or buried. Both actions will mark the spell complete.

You can also perform this as a healing ritual for yourself.

A Group Brigid Rite of Healing

When troubled times hit a community, this rite for group healing can help soothe ragged souls. After the bombing at the Boston Marathon, a number of us came together to do a similar ritual for the healing of those impacted by it. As with any group rite, modifications for the specific group will likely need to be made.

Materials

A vessel of water—large enough to anoint all, small enough to carry around the room comfortably. Mix the water with salt, lavender, a small portion of milk, and honey.

One large candle for the altar and a tea light candle for each person attending.

An altar table decorated with red, green, and white (ribbons, cloths, etc.).

St. Brigid's crosses, Brigid statues, or a picture of Brigid (can be downloaded from the Internet). You don't need a ton of items, but simply something evocative of Brigid will be beneficial to your work.

If the ritual is for a specific person or group of people needing healing, place trinkets belonging to them on the altar.

Assemble guests in a circle around the room. Candles should be unlit at the beginning. Cast sacred space either through a method comfortable and accessible to those present or in the previous Brigid circle casting. Guests at the rite, one at a time, should take hands. When the sacred space is set, a ritual leader petitions Brigid:

"Brigid, Lady of the Wells—we invite you now to our space to heal (recipient). Brigid, Lady of the Bards, help our words and *work inspire healing for* (recipient). *Brigid, Lady of the Smiths, give us the strength to support* (recipient) *while* (he/she/they) *take(s) this journey of healing."*

A ritual leader holds up the bowl of water and says, *"Brigid, from the depths of your Sacred Well, people found healing. We call upon that heart of Water, the cooling purifying force to heal* (recipient) *and all those who love and support* (him/her/them)." The leader then walks around the room, anointing each person with the water from the bowl, lastly sprinkling water from the vessel onto the trinkets on the altar.

For a few moments, guests meditate on a vision of healing for the recipient.

A ritual leader lights the large candle on the altar and offers the following incantation: *"Sacred Brigid, for many centuries your daughters tended your flame for nineteen nights. On the twentieth night, they surrendered it to your care and you tended it alone. We children assemble now—this is our nineteenth night in Spirit. We light these flames, but surrender (recipient) to your care for healing."*

Individually, guests light tea light candles from the main flame and set them on the altar. This is a good opportunity for individuals to offer personal prayers or intentions.

A ritual leader comes forward and says, *"Brigid, Lady of the Bards, accept our offerings of inspiration to sing the soul of (recipient) to healing."*

This is a good time for guests to offer songs, poems, or other creative contributions, if they would like.

At the end of the rite, a leader announces that the ritual is closed. A final song or "om" should be offered, with all participants envisioning the energy traveling to the recipient. Light food or drink should be shared for fellowship and grounding.

BRIGID SPELLS FOR CREATORS

For creative endeavors, the following spells can coax stubborn ideas out of uninspired minds. A few can help motivate projects to full fruition while others can help add creative spice to your productive life if it's gotten a bit bland.

A Brigid Spell for Inspiration

This simple spell is based on the one I first used to ask Brigid for help writing. It is also the one I suggested to blocked writers who came to a SoHo restaurant where I once worked, when they asked for "witchy" help.

Materials

Basic Brigid oil

Three red candles

A pinch of cinnamon

The size of the candle depends on the work you want to do. I like to use the small, two-hour taper candles, which are commonly found at occult shops. The small candles give me just enough of a "boost" of inspiration to move forward on my own. Votives are fine, if those are easier to obtain. If you're dealing with a serious creative block and need a bigger push, a seven-day candle might be in order. The color of the candle is important. Red invokes the power and image of the forge-creator and the heart of the Bard. Orange is an okay substitute, but red is your best bet. Again, some spells will encourage you to leave a candle burning until it has ended. Unless you plan to spend seven days at home in twenty-four hour stints, do not do this, and do not leave your candles burning unattended.

As Brigid works in triplicate, it is best to use three candles.

Mix a small portion of your Brigid oil with the pinch of cinnamon. Set your sacred space and spend a few moments in silence. Acknowledge the thoughts that come to you, but do not follow them, analyze them, or try too hard to push them away. Stay in as much of a space of quiet as you are able, knowing you are creating space in your mind for inspiration to arrive.

When you feel you have created the space, hold one candle (unlit) with the base touching your heart and anoint the candle with Brigid oil (wick first), pulling it toward you and saying, *"Brigid, inspire my heart."*

Take the second candle, this time with the base at your throat and anoint as before saying, *"Brigid, inspire my voice."*

Take the third candle with the base at your forehead, anoint and say, *"Brigid, inspire my mind."*

Set the three candles in your sacred space and light the wicks. Offer a personal prayer to Brigid for the inspiration you want to receive. Inspiration might not strike in the moment you light the candles, but in the days to come you will find new ideas coming to you. Seize them when they come up as no idea sticks around unattended for long!

When the candles have burned down completely, be sure to make offerings in thanks for the inspiration, even before it arrives. Tea, biscuits, or a mug of beer on your altar/sacred space can help move the energy into that of celebrating a success. I've also seen that when those using Brigid Magick to create dedicate a monetary portion of their success to a charity or someone in need, their future successes increase dramatically.

Opening the Paths Spell

This spell is designed for increased creativity and to bring new opportunities your way. I dreamed this spell, and tried it the next day. I received an incredible burst of ideas in the days that followed.

Materials

Six white roses

A sprig of lavender

Charged Brigid Water (Note: Leaving a cup of water in your sacred Brigid space will charge it on its own. You will want to change it regularly to keep it fresh. If you do not have a space to keep Brigid Water, you can hold your hands over the water, speaking a prayer to Brigid, until you feel your hands throb.)

In your sacred space, arrange the six roses and lavender as though they were a flowering tree. It will help expand ideas you have on your mental percolator and bring in new ones, too. Sprinkle the flowers with the Brigid Water. Here's how I typically do so.

If possible, leave the flowers in the position until they dry out. Collect the petals and keep in a sachet, squeezing the sachet when you are in need of inspiration. If you cannot leave the flowers out, go ahead and gather the petals into the sachet when you are finished with the spell. Discard stems in a garden or park.

The Last Sheaf: For Continued Success

This is another version of the Brídeog tradition. As an American, I struggled with this spell. I do not want to appropriate a cultural tradition, yet could not ignore the inspiration the practice gave me. Sometimes spells grab hold and won't let us rest until they come to paper. I write this with credence to the inspiration of the Brídeog, but not with the intention of re-creating or re-inventing it.

When a project has been completed, a major deal closed, or a prosperous fiscal year has wrapped, take a biodegradable token of that endeavor and wrap it in the dried-out sheaf or particles of your area's local crop. I live in New York, where some of our primary crops include corn and apples, so I might use a corn sheaf or a dried out apple skin. If your local crop is particularly juicy, such as mango, take extra time to dry the skin or vines so that you don't end up with a mess. The token might be a business card, a copy of an offer letter, or a flier or program from a production, if you are a performer. If you collaborated with a number of people, you might want to ask them to join you as this is a particularly strong practice for groups.

Placing your hands on the sheaf, speak aloud all things for which you were grateful to have come to you through this endeavor. Keep the sheaf in your home for a night. If you worked with others, pass the sheaf along to another person on your team for them to keep for a night (hence why drying the sheaves or skins is so important) and have them do the same—giving thanks to the bounty you all have enjoyed.

The sheaf should be buried in a garden or park, with appropriate biodegradable or energetic offering left behind.

BRIGID HOME PROTECTION MAGICK: HOW TO CHARM YOUR HOUSE WITH BRIGID

The St. Brigid's cross was traditionally fixed to houses and stables in the belief that St. Brigid would protect the occupants— both human and animal—from harm. Illness was a primary concern, although house fires were an equally serious and common threat in a time when fires were the main sources of heat and light in a home. St. Brigid's crosses and the following incantation listed were believed to protect a home from fire:

> *An' if perhaps you do admire,*
> *That this great house did ne'er take fire,*
> *Where sparks, as thick as stars in sky,*
> *About the house did often fly,*
> *And reach'd the sapless wither'd thatch,*
> *Which dry like spunge the fire would catch,*
> *And where no chimney was erected,*
> *Where sparks and flames might be directed,*
> *St. Bridget's cross hung over door,*
> *Which did the house from fire secure,*
> *As Gillo thought, O powerful charm*
> *To keep a house from taking harm:*
> *And tho' the dogs and servants slept,*
> *by Bridget's care the house was kept.*

St. Brigid's crosses are easy to come by in occult stores or even many church gift shops. You can also make your own, the instructions for which can be found in Chapter 8. One very easy method of bringing permanent Brigid energy to your house is to include the cross while painting the walls of your house. When it is time for a fresh coat of paint, start out by painting the cross onto the wall, before covering it up with the rest of the paint. It won't show when the work is complete, but the energy will be present.

Consider making use of the prayer above to enchant the St. Brigid's crosses to protective life. Its antiquity will give it strength. It will serve as a calling card to Brigid to let her know you wish your home to be under her protection. Reinforce these words annually, perhaps as part of your Imbolc rites, to keep them strong and firm.

BRIGID'S LOVE MAGICK

Brigid has been in the magickal match-making business for quite some time. Perhaps it is being the Patroness of the house and home, but even St. Brigid kept busy finding husbands for devout Catholic women. A prayer (that sounds quite like a spell to me . . .) involves a young woman seeking marriage lighting a candle in the church and reciting the following:

Holy St. Brigid and Blessed St. Anne,
Get me a man as fast as you can.

Surely, this could be augmented to suit the gender(s) of your own desires and the practice could take place at your own sacred space.

Being a Patroness of hearth and home, Brigid Magick is finely attuned to partnership, more so than short-term flingish arrangements. Invoke Brigid Magick for love when you are ready for a life partnership or if you want to enhance the stability of an existing relationship. Brigid will often send along matches we might not normally expect that ultimately provide what we most need. I could write a library's worth of materials detailing the love spells I have performed that went terribly, terribly wrong before I met my partner. Among many things I credit to our meeting, one was the spell I did to Brigid to find love. It was also the simplest spell I've performed. One day, I looked at my Brigid altar and said, "Brigid, I know he's out there. Bring him along." A few months later, I met him.

The following spells can help move that process along, as well.

A Brigid Love Oil

Materials

Base: almond oil.

5 parts rose hips essential oil, 4 parts passionflower essential oil, 2 parts basil essential oil

Rose water (Note: You can make your own rose water by simmering the petals and pollen of several roses in a couple of inches of water. Brigid loves white roses, but given the connection with red roses and romance, a combination of the two might be perfect. Petals, stems, or other pollen pieces should be removed from the water and the water should be stored in the refrigerator. Discard after a couple of months as it will grow rancid.)

2 parts lavender essential oil

3 parts patchouli essential oil

1 part vanilla extract

2 parts mugwort essential oil

If you made the basic Brigid oil, using it as a base for this spell will be beautifully effective.

The oil can be made whenever it is convenient for you, but should be dedicated to Brigid at dawn. As with the inspiration spell, concoct your love oil with an open mind. Brigid's love magick does not take well to dictation. Casting for the affections of a specific person or a too-detailed description of a hypothetical person is likely to backfire as again, Brigid is known for giving spell casters exactly what they ask for, only for them to learn that it is exactly what they *don't* want. The best course of action is to define what *kind* of love you are looking for, which might take some serious self-searching prior to casting. I cannot recommend enough leaving the choice in Brigid's hands, although I say this with the understanding that this can be a tough thing to do.

This oil is great for attracting people of all genders, as its components are generally pleasing to most people. Wearing a bit to a club or party is likely to draw you plenty of wanted attention, but its Brigid energy will help filter out whether the attention is in line with the kind of love you are seeking. Again, don't use this potion if you are looking for something casual. Brigid love magick is built for long-term arrangements.

You can also burn this oil on candles, incorporating the symbol of fiery passion into your magick. Red candles have a natural connection to love. Pink, yellow, or white inspire love and connection. If you'd like, select a combination. Anoint them as performed in the Inspiration Spell above, but anoint each one toward your heart, in turn by holding the candle with its base toward your heart and applying the oil by starting at the wick of the candle and pulling the oil and energy toward you. Burn the candles in complete confidence that your spell is working and that Brigid will bring the love that is best for you.

If You Need to End a Long-Term Relationship . . .

Likewise, if you need to separate yourself from a relationship that is failing but can't seem to end, use three blue candles (for cooling energies), and anoint them from the heart area in reverse (starting at the base and pushing the oil and energy outward, away from you). As the candles burn, meditate on what went right in the relationship and what went wrong. Bless the mistakes and lessons and embrace forward movement.

To Restore Love and Harmony to a Partnership

A man came to Brigid in a state of despair. His wife claimed she no longer loved him and threatened to leave him. He begged Brigid for a spell to make his wife love him again. Brigid blessed some water and gave it to him, instructing him to sprinkle it over their house, food, drink, and over their bed. He returned home and performed the act. His wife suddenly became exceedingly loving and wanted to be with him all the time. The marriage was saved and the couple praised Brigid.

—TRADITIONAL TALE

Materials

Rose petals—red, white, pink, or a combination

Fresh or dried lavender

Sea salt

Three large, very red apples split down the middle

Honey

Fresh milk

Note: *This spell is based on the myth above.*

Prepare a bath for yourself, placing rose petals, lavender, sea salt, and apples in the water. Soak in the water alongside these elements with the lights off. Periodically pour the water over your head and rub your limbs, heart, and head with the apples. Focus on what you love about the relationship and what parts of it you would like to see enhanced or restored. Painful memories or anger may surface—if this happens, acknowledge the thoughts but don't dwell on them. If you find you cannot get past anger or pain enough to meditate on the good things about your loved one, you may need to try the bath again later or reconsider performing the spell altogether.

When you feel full of love, hope, and potential for your relationship, collect a large bowl of the water from the bath before emptying the tub. Mix a few drops of honey and a few drops of fresh milk into the bathwater and mix well. Only use a couple of drops of milk or it will sour and *no* relationship can thrive in a house that smells like sour milk. Recite the following:

> Brigid, melt the ice
> Brigid, warm and thaw,
> Brigid heal (name of significant other)'s heart,
> Mend our home and hearth.

The intention is for complete healing of the relationship—not for the other person to see things "your" way, or to change their behavior, attitude, or personality to be something you desire. Complete healing between two parties will mean you will also be asked, either by your partner or through synchronicity, to evaluate how you can better support the relationship. Also, be prepared that sometimes the best way to soothe a relationship is to end it, which this spell could do if the relationship is irreparable. However, Brigid Magick often sees things to an amicable completion.

One possible note of caution for this spell . . .

In another version of the above myth, the wife became so re-infatuated with her husband that she couldn't stand to even be even as far from him as across the room, which annoyed the man so much he went to sea. The wife stood on the shores wailing day and night until he came back. While I haven't seen yet the spell invoke such powers of obsession, that version may contain a warning!

Amulet to Protect a Love Affair

Materials

A piece of paper.

A trinket given to you by your beloved—it must be given to you by their own volition. You cannot take it from them.

Red thread.

A jar and honey.

An odd-numbered combination of herbs sacred to Brigid (see list above for reference) that are to your liking and, to your knowledge, to the liking of your beloved.

Write your name and the name(s) of your beloved so that they are crossing each other. If you can make it so that the names form a St. Brigid's cross, even better! If you are not that crafty, simply having the letters intersect will be sufficient. Wrap the paper around the trinket you received and bind the whole thing with red thread until the entire bundle is wrapped in it. Place the bundle in the jar and cover it with the herbs and honey, gluing the lid tightly on.

Say the following words as you hold the jar tightly, imbuing it with the powers of preservation. Focus on the beauty of the relationship and what you wish to see develop from it:

Brig is Come, Brig is Welcome,
Brig is Come, Brig is Welcome.
Brigid of Power, Brigid of Light,
Join and help me here this night.
But no harsh words be uttered,
No timing be off,
No passions go dimmer,
No hearts shall be scoffed.

Brigid, be gentle, Brigid be kind,
Breathe life to this love, this sweet love of mine.

Say these phrases while grasping the amulet until you feel your hands throb.

Keep this amulet in a secret place. This is not recommended for struggling relationships, but rather new ones with great potential or long-term ones looking to maintain a positive status quo.

BRIGID'S MONEY MAGICK

The Perpetual Butter Spell

When Brigid was a grown girl, the Druid and his wife went one day to the dairy where their daughter was helping her mother and demanded to have a great hamper, eighteen hands high, to be filled with butter. Brigid had only the making of one churning and a half but, at her prayer, the butter increased so that if the hampers of the men of Munster had been given to her, Brigid would have filled them all.

—Traditional tale

Once again, symbolic items help bring out the things you wish to manifest. If you are short on funds, write down the exact amount of money you need to close that cash gap. Fill a small bowl with fresh butter and mix with clover, oak acorns (if you have them in your region), and dandelion pollen. Clover is meant for luck, oak represents strength and protection, and dandelion pollen is used because dandelions can grow pretty much anywhere! All of these elements can help a tough money situation. Place the paper in the center of the butter and say the following:

Eighteen hands high and I of nigh have none,
So it is written, so it is done,
I shall have bounty aplenty
By Brigid's good graces, my pockets ne'er empty.

Keep the butter in a cool place so it will not spoil, until the money comes to be. Then, melt butter and pour on the crossroads (or intersection) to invite the money to keep coming back!

Working with the Bacon Sachet

This spell is reminiscent of the story of Brigid feeding bacon to the hungry dog, which can be found in Chapter 9. Another Brigid custom stemming from County Limerick is the hanging of a small bag containing three slices of bacon along with the St. Brigid's cross over the main door on Imbolc Eve to encourage prosperity within the household throughout the year. It is not clear why the myth focuses on five slices of bacon while the practice only uses three, although the story comes from the canon of Brigid the Saint, and the number three has profound significance in Celtic Christianity. Brigid the Saint, as discussed earlier in the book, was known for her abundant giving. This is reminiscent of her earliest roots as a land Goddess and, in this myth, the prosperous face of the Earth.

The following practice is less a traditional spell and more of a practice and personal pilgrimage. To know the blessings of Brigid, channel the Spirit of the Earth Mother herself. Give every day, particularly if what you give is akin to something you need. When we give of ourselves what we also desire for ourselves, that energy is returned in abundance.

Materials

Slips of paper or small but significant trinkets that represent the blessings you have in your life along with blessings you wish to receive.

A small bag or cloth.

A special place to hang the bag or bound bundle. Over a doorway, particularly a main entryway, is ideal. If you cannot do that, tucking it into a more discreet place, such as under a bed or in a personal tote bag is also fine.

If you are using paper instead of trinkets, list your blessings, along with individual things you want to manifest, on individual pieces. Bundle the papers or the trinkets into the bag or cloth and hang or store as suggested above. Select one at random every morning as something you plan to give so far as you are able. As an example, if you happen to be blessed with money or if you need to bring more money to your household, contribute money throughout the day where needed as you are able. Maybe you're in a position where you can purchase lunch for a friend, or maybe you're in a position where you can only give a little bit to a charity you like. If you do not have money in abundance and money is something you desire, consider donating time, barter, or assistance to those who are also in need. The intent and energy will be the same and in time, the abundance you seek will grow. Matters get trickier when the desired blessing might be something like sex. If you want sexual intimacy in your life, or if you feel your sexual life is a true blessing you enjoy, simply going out and offering sex wherever you go would likely cross a lot of inappropriate boundaries. However, the desire to feel attractive is universal. Find ways to show others their beautiful worth in a way that is respectful and sensitive to personal boundaries. The same shall be returned to you, in time.

When the bag is empty, thank Brigid for the opportunity to share and enjoy your gifts as they are returned to you. The key is to give without agenda. Do not look for thanks, recognition, or the like. Wait for the blessings to unfold. Do not dictate what kind of blessings you want to receive. Enjoy their unique manifestations.

OTHER BRIGID SPELLS

The Brigid Magpie Spell

We are humans. Therefore, we do not always get along. Brigid herself didn't even get along with everyone! The following spell is useful during those times when you don't wish someone harm, but might wish them many pleasant distractions . . . as far away from you as possible.

Materials

Name or photograph of person you want to go away. If feasible, and if you are comfortable going to this length, their hair and/or nail clippings are helpful, too.

Several pieces of paper. Each piece of paper should list something you know would make the person happy. If you cannot think of anything (some people truly love misery!), all-purpose items would include money or love.

A jar of honey.

A dollop of glitter.

Stick the first two items listed into a jar of honey with the glitter. Shake the jar, envisioning the person as having all of these things manifest for them. Then, imagine these things happening to the person in a region far from you. Say the following:

May Brigid grant you love,
May Brigid grant you health,
May Brigid grant you strength,
May Brigid grant you wealth,
May you see these things and more,
Enough to fill the sea,
Brigid grant you blessings,
far away from me.

Throw the jar away in a garbage can on the other side of town. Even better, drive a few hours and leave it in a garbage can in a whole new area. For truly rough cases, consider mailing it to someone on another continent.

"Caught at Crossroads" Magick

Brigid may not be automatically known for patronage of crossroads, but the home threshold holds the same power as the crossroads, which is believed by many traditions to be a liminal place of great magick, as does the doorway. For the purpose of this work, let us draw from the idea of standing with a foot in two worlds, akin to Brigid's mother standing in the doorway, or the Dagda or the Morrighan straddling the river. This spell can be used for circumstances in which the best course of direction is unclear.

This working should take place in a doorway of your home.

Materials

A symbolic object for each course of direction or one piece of paper with each potential course written on it. Photographs evocative of the different courses would work well also.

A candle, the color of which should identify with your dilemma (a red candle for a matter of the heart, a green candle for a matter of business, etc.). Do not use a "dripless" candle. The melted wax is important to the work.

A plate, tray, or other dish that will not be damaged by the candle's heat or the melted wax.

It is important that this spell be completed at sunrise.

Set the different symbols of the choices on either side of the doorframe. If you are battling with more than two choices (Goddess forbid!), set the symbols in balanced space from one another. Sit in the doorway, the symbols on either side of you. Breathe deeply and sit in the quiet dark with your dilemma, acknowledging all parts of it and potential outcomes. Be sure you are ready to make a choice. Offer a private prayer to Brigid regarding the situation. Because of the deeply personal nature of crossroads magick, I chose not to include a pre-written incantation. If you are performing this spell, take this time to be very present with your situation and with Brigid's direct guidance.

When you are ready, light the candle and sit in silence with the flame. As the candle drips down, observe where the wax travels. You may decide to get up and go about business in the house while the candle burns. This is fine, but again—do not leave the candle fully unattended! When the candle has burned completely down and away, take a look at where the wax ran. If it pooled in the direction of one choice more than the other, you have received your answer. If the wax pooled in equal directions or if it is unclear, the time is not right to make a decision. Give the spell some time, perhaps a few weeks, and try again if the decision is still difficult.

Brigid's Breath: A Revival Spell

This simple spell restores energy to lackluster times, endeavors, or relationships. It can also be a gentle springtime rite in preparation for shedding winter doldrums.

Materials

A charm, stone, or other amulet that can either be worn or tucked into a pocket for regular use

On the first day feeling remotely like spring, go outside and rub the amulet on the earth. Wear or carry the charm around for the first few weeks of spring, particularly in situations were extra revitalization may be required.

A Fertility Spell

Fertility spells are often transformed into other types of spells: "fertilizing" the social circle to enhance personal relationships, or "fertilizing" job prospects and, in many cases, this works. The following spell, however, is intended for those who do wish to conceive children and its transmutation to another purpose is not recommended.

Materials

A cradle either for a doll or a human child

A babydoll (optional)

Some variations of the practice have the person desiring a child to put the babydoll in the cradle. Other variations use an empty cradle. This is a personal choice. Some people do not like dolls, but others may appreciate the visual representation. Either way, the cradle should be rocked and the following spoken aloud.

O Bride, come with the wand
To this wintry land,

And breathe with the breath of Spring so bland,
Bride, Bride, little Bride...

This spell is best performed in the evening, just prior to bedtime.

Spell for Brigid's Justice

Materials

Three gold candles. (If this spell is for justice for a bodily injury, use red candles instead of gold.)

Six gold (or golden) coins. Use your country's currency. In the United States, we have $1 gold coins, which are great for this purpose. They can be obtained at a bank. If your country does not produce a golden coin, find something as close to it as possible.

On a piece of paper, write the description of the situation needing justice—what went wrong, what needs to be rectified. This is called a petition. If you have a photograph of the situation (such as damage to a home or car), writing your petition on the image is very powerful. Set the petition on top of the six gold coins and arrange the candles around it. Sprinkle with a blend of black pepper and soil from a local courthouse, along with a pinch of soil from the land you live on. Light the candles and say the following:

Brigid of the Well, wash away adversity.
Brigid of the Anvil, fortify my armor.
Brigid of the Bard, sing songs of my victory.
Justice be served! Justice be Right! Justice be Swift!
Brigid, go forth and conquer for me!

Pierce through the effigy with the iron nail. Burn candles around this image for at least an hour, replacing the candles as necessary for nineteen consecutive nights. On the twentieth, do not burn candles, and say the lines above again, replacing the last line with *Brigid, this Task now belongs to You.*

To Bring Truth and Light to a Situation

This spell is best used if you can light a fire.

Materials

9 acorns or 9 twigs of oak, or a combination

Write the nature of the blocked situation on a paper, and wrap it around the bundle of oak or acorns. While embracing the bundle, focus on the situation for which you need clarity until you feel your temples could burst from the focus. Call out the following:

Oak! Open the door!
Brigid the Warrior, light the way!
Shine your fire into the shadow,
Spear and Sword of Truth, chase out the putrid!
Truth shall prevail!
Truth shall prevail!
Truth shall prevail!

Toss the bundle into the fire. There is no shortcut to this working. If you do not have a fireplace or fire pit, you will need to seek one out. The working will also require sacrifice of your own kind—either money or time to a cause promoting justice.

A Road-Opener Spell with Brigid

Take a green apple and write on it (a permanent marker helps) the things that are hindering you. This spell is best designed for internal blocks, such as personal insecurities or fears. If you need to eliminate a block occurring outside of you, such as nepotism in your place of work or school, write "nepotism" on the apple. Don't write the actual names of the persons, if any, who are causing the problem. Some believe this would be a form of baneful magick. My experience has been that spells work best when they address specific aspects of the situation, more so than the persons manifesting it. Take time to think about what the actual problem involves while holding the apple. Concentrate until you feel the actual apple buzz in your hands. Say the following:

> *Brigid! Lend your spear!*
> *Brigid! Lend your shield!*
> *Bring forth fire's fury and the river's force,*
> *The Oak's strength, and the Warrior's Glory,*
> *I break these chains, I sever these bonds,*
> *I am triumphant! I am Brigantia-Victoria!*

Smash the apple with a hammer or hurl it against a tree. Don't be afraid to really pummel the fruit—stomping and grinding underfoot could be helpful as well. When the apple has been thoroughly demolished, collect any seeds that remain and carry them in a pocket or as a talisman when going in to the work that needs to be done.

IT IS IMPORTANT TO REMEMBER . . .

Go into your work with pure heart and intention. Brigid's Magick does not respond well to vindictive qualities, jealousy, or overt greed. It is okay to cast spells for things that please you and give you joy, even if you don't really *need* the things you seek. But be sure to take time to reflect on these things before casting. Will the things you cast for bring you true fulfillment? Or are they motivated by a desire for power over others for power's own sake? Brigid's myths include numerous instances of her cursing those who refused to help others or who wielded power unfairly. But her stories also tell of bountiful blessings to those who seek her magick with pure desire for manifesting positive change in themselves or others. Don't approach Brigid's Magick in fear of "doing it wrong," or "invoking Brigid's wrath." Approach it after honest reflection of the true nature of the desire has taken place. Beautiful things will manifest as a result.

Magick is a practice—not an order to the Universe in the way you might order food delivery. Spell casters in consumer communities often struggle with this. "I cast a spell. I should get what I asked for." I see this quite often, unfortunately. It frustrates the spell caster and undermines the spell. No one is entitled to a long-lasting relationship, exorbitant riches, or anything for the mere want of it. Yet, there is nothing wrong with casting a spell for any of these things. It is important to understand, however, that the practice of magick is the energetic contribution to the desired intentions as though the work were planting things in a garden. Some things will turn up as you expected, but there is no way to truly know the shape of the individual flower until it blooms. Brigid's Magick requires the diligence and strength of the work on the forge, the patience of the still waters of the well, and absorption of the genuine fulfillment found in a solid loaf of fresh bread.

Good luck and blessed be!

Epilogue

St. Brigid's flame in the Market Square in Kildaretown. The flame monument was unveiled on February 1, 2006, by Ireland's President of that time, Mary McAleese. Photo and text courtesy of Elizabeth Guerra-Walker.

Early in my Brigid journey, I wondered if I should have picked a different Goddess to devote so much of my spiritual journey to, perhaps one more obscure so I wouldn't be just one more drop in a Brigid ocean. It seemed as though everywhere I went, I ran into self-described daughters and sons of Brigid—among Pagans, Christians, and more. Brigid was everywhere. Was I only following a trend? Should I have done more searching before claiming this Goddess as my own personal guide? Would I have found deeper mysteries and greater knowledge in a lesser-known Goddess? In time, that didn't matter. I grew to love the breadth, depth, and myriad of ways Brigid is revered and the fact that I was part of something so big and beautiful, the expanse of how she continues to be worshipped.

Brigid is a litany: the Healer, the Smith, the Mother, the Dawn, the Warrior, the Poet. Most of all, she is permanent. Will we eventually see incarnations of Brigid colonizing space? Probably. Will time look back on her as part of the inspiration for a green-technology revolution? It's quite possible. If anything, this book has hopefully revealed just how much life and spirit continues to be poured into Brigid and through her, how much is then rebirthed into the world. Brigid did not fade and become revitalized. She adapted. She holds too tight on the corner of humanity's soul to be simply whipped away by the winds of time. She has become part of our collective soul's fabric, certainly growing even stronger with the centuries.

First and always, she is a Goddess of life. This doesn't mean that working with her will always be pleasant. Life has war, pain, the sometimes-difficult journey of healing, the sweat and frustration and even failures of work and loss. Even death itself is an integral part of life. But even so, life also contains joy, laughter, astounding beauty, the thrill of accomplishment—a glorious mixture of all and then some.

Your Brigid journey will be much the same. Take the tough moments with laughter, savor the gentle gems. Keep record of the synchronistic moments as they arise. Brigid has no blanket code of conduct. How she will speak to and manifest for you will be unique to you, alone. It is my hope that this book has provided some tools to connect mysterious dots and point out a few doorways. It will be up to you to approach these doorways and see what patterns these dots actually make. Above all:

May your forge be ever ready
May your hammer be ever strong
May each dawn bring you new hope
May your armor be always prepared
May Her White Cow be at your side
Wherever your journey take you across this green Earth,
May Brigid always light the way.

Blessed be your journey, friend. Thank you for reading.

Acknowledgments

My most sincere thanks to all who contributed their resources, information, and assistance: Lisa Bleviss, Mael Brigde, George and Yvonne Courtney, James Demartis, Janet Farrar and Gavin Bone, Valerie Fresemen, Selena Fox, Michael Graham, Elizabeth Guerra-Walker, Professor Ronald Hutton, the Rev. Dr. Queen Mother Imakhu, Awen Luna, Lee Morgan, Mark Snowsowski, Liz Williams and Trevor Jones, Carey A. Moore, Nanci Moy, Hector Luis Siri, the people of County Meath, Ireland, and the New York Public Library. To my editor Amber Guetebier and team at Weiser Books for this opportunity. For writer and editing support from Reverend Jen Miller, Michele Carlo, Jennifer Glick, Jennifer DeMerritt, Hilary Parry, and Ivo Dominguez, Jr. For the tours, the blessed gems in the guise of stories, and the preservation of these glorious sites, my thanks to the people at the parish of St. Brigid and St. Emeric and the committee that saved this Church in New York, NY; the parishes at St. Bridget's Church at St. Bride's Bay; St. Bridget's Church, Skenfrith; St. Bridget's Church, Chelvey; the Church of St. Bridget, Dyserth; Church of St. Ffraid, Trearddur Bay; the Cathedral Church of St. Brigid, Kildare; Sister Mary Minehan and the Sisters at the Solas Bhríde Centre and Hermitage. To Neil Gaiman, Amanda Palmer, and Tori Amos for inspiring me through words and song. I can't wait to one day tell you how much in person. For their introduction to and co-exploration into this remarkable Goddess: Lady Cyn and Fern DeFay, Megan Bridget Flanagan, Isabell Rolon, and the Novices of the Old Ways and the Lunar Temple. To my family, Patti and Eric Weber, Meredith, Nate and Westley Gordon, and my best friend Tiffany Jean. A very special thanks Gemma McGowan for the ever-constant support, information, time, driving skills, and helping me stitch all the confusing pieces into something that made sense. Finally, with thanks and love to my partner Brian, for his support and patience and above all, for saying I could when I said could not.

Bibliography

BOOKS

Aldhouse-Green, Miranda. *Caesar's Druids: Story of an Ancient Priesthood.* Yale University Press, New Haven and London. 2010.

Berger, Pamela. *The Goddess Obscured.* Beacon Press, Boston. 1985.

Bitel, Lisa M. *Landscape with Two Saints: How Genovefa of Paris and Brigit of Kildaire Built Christianity in Barbarian Europe.* Oxford University Press, Oxford. 2009.

Condren, Mary. *The Serpent and the Goddess: Women, Religion and Power in Celtic Ireland.* New Island Books, Dublin. 2002.

Ellis, Peter Berresford. *The Celtic Empire: The First Millennium of Celtic History 1000 BC–AD 51.* Carroll & Graf Publishers, New York. 1990.

Ellis, Peter Berresford. *Celtic Myths and Legends.* Running Press Book Publishers, Philadelphia, Pennsylvania. 2002.

Ellis, Peter Berresford. *Celtic Women: Women in Celtic Soicety and Literature.* Constable and Company Limited, London. 1995.

Ellis, Peter Berresford. *The Druids.* William B. Eerdmans Publishing Company, Grand Rapids, Michigan. 1994.

Evans, William. *Bards of the Isle of Britain: An Inquiry into Their History and the Validity of Their Records and Traditions.*

Published by the Author at Peny Bond, Red Wharf Bay, Anglesey. 1930.

Farrar, Janet and Stewart. *The Witches' Goddess*. Phoenix Publishing, Inc., Custer, Washington. 1987.

Freeman, Philip. *War, Women, and Druids: Eyewitness Reports and Early Accounts of the Ancient Celts*. University of Texas Press, Austin. 2002.

Gibson, George Cinclain. *Wake Rites: The Ancient Irish Rituals for 'Finnegan's Wake.'* University Press of Florida, Gainesville. 2005.

Hutton, Ronald. *Blood and Mistletoe: The History of the Druids in Britain*. Yale University Press, New Haven and London. 2011.

Hutton, Ronald. *The Pagan Religions of the Ancient British Isles: Their Nature and Legacy*. Blackwell Publishing, Malden, Massachusetts. 1993.

Joyce, P.W. *Old Celtic Romances*. Wordsworth Editions in association with the Folklore Society, London. 2000.

Kondratiev, Alexei. *Celtic Rituals: An Authentic Guide to Ancient Celtic Spirituality*. New Celtic Publishing, Scotland. 1999.

Lady Gregory's Complete Irish Mythology. Bounty Books, London. 2004.

Laing, Lloyd. *Celtic Britain*. Routledge & Kegan Paul, London and Henley. 1979.

Laing, Lloyd and Jennifer. *Celtic Britain and Ireland*. Irish Academic Press, Dublin. 1990.

MacKillop, James. *Myths and Legends of the Celts*. Penguin Books, London. 2005.

MacNeill, Máire. *The Festival of Lughnasa*. Comhairle Bhéaloideas Éireann, University College, Dublin. 2008.

Miles, Dillwyn. *Secrets of the Bards of the Isle of Britain*. Gwasy Dinefwr Press, Dyfed, Wales. 1992.

Minehan, Rita, CSB. *Rekindling the Flame: A Pilgrimage in the Footsteps of Brigid of Kildare.* Solas Bhríde Community, Kildare, Ireland. 1999.

Moffat, Alistair. *The Sea Kingdoms.* HarperCollins, London. 2001.

Ó Catháin, Séamas. *The Festival of Brigit: Celtic Goddess and Holy Woman.* DBA Publications, Ltd, Blackrock. 1995.

Ó Duinn, Seán. *The Rites of Brigid, Goddess and Saint.* The Columba Press, Dublin. 2004.

Ó Duinn, Seán. *Where Three Streams Meet: Celtic Spirituality.* The Columba Press, Dublin. 2000.

Rolleston, T.W. *Celtic Myths and Legends.* Dover Publications, Inc., New York. 1990.

Ross, Anne. *The Everyday Life of the Pagan Celts.* B.T. Batsford, Ltd., London; G.P. Putnam's Sons, New York. 1970.

Ross, Anne and Don Robins. *The Life and Death of a Druid Prince.* Summit Books, New York. 1989.

Spence, Lewis. *The Magic Arts in Celtic Britain.* Rider and Company, London. 1947.

Squire, Charles. *Mythology of the Celtic People.* Bracken Books, London. 1997.

Stewart, R.J. *Celtic Bards, Celtic Druids.* Blandford A. Cassell Imprint, London. 1996.

Stewart, R.J. *Celtic Gods, Celtic Goddesses.* Cassell Illustrated, London. 2006.

Smucker, Anna Egan. *The Life of St. Brigid.* Appletree Press, Belfast. 2007.

Haitian Vodou. Llewellyn Publications, Woodbury, Minnesota. 2012.

Thomas, Charles. *Celtic Britain.* Thames and Hudson, Inc. New York. 1986.

Thompson, Jack George. *Women in Celtic Law and Culture.* The Edwin Mellen Press, Limited. Lampeter, Dyfed, Wales. 1996.

Uris, Leon. *Trinity.* Doubleday & Company, Inc. Garden City, New York. 1976.

Wait, Gerald A. *Ritual and Religion in Iron Age Britain: Part I.* BAR British Series, Oxford. 1985.

Webster Wilde, Lyn. *Celtic Women in Legend, Myth and History.* Wellington House, London. 1997.

Williams, Carolyn D. *Boudica and her Stories: Narrative Transformations of a Warrior Queen.* Rosemont Publishing and Printing. Company. Cranbury, New Jersey. 2009.

Wright, Brian. *Brigid: Goddess, Druidess and Saint.* The History Press. Stroud, Gloucestershire. 2009.

CHANTS, CDS, OTHER ONLINE RESOURCES

A Dream Whose Time Is Coming. Assembly of the Sacred Wheel: *www.sacredwheel.org*

Chants: Ritual Music from Reclaiming and Friends. *www .serpentinemusic.com*

La Lugh: Brighid's Kiss. *celticgrooves.homestead.com/CG_La _Lugh_Brighid.html*

Chants, rituals, and other Brigid material courtesy of Circle Sanctuary are available online at *www.circlesanctuary.org*, *circlepodcasts.org*, and *www.selenafox.com*

Artist Carey A. Moore's work can be found at *www.odyssey craftworks.com*

Index

About the Author

Courtney Weber is a priestess, writer, Tarot advisor, activist, and practicing witch in New York City. Her writing has appeared in several publications and she blogs at *www.thecocowitch.com* and on *www.witchesandpagans.com* ("Behind the Broom: What the Books Don't Tell You"). She is the designer and producer of *Tarot of the Boroughs*, a photographic Tarot deck set in New York City. Courtney lectures regularly around the United States and travels to Ireland frequently, leading tours of the sacred sites.

To Our Readers

Weiser Books, an imprint of Red Wheel/Weiser, publishes books across the entire spectrum of occult, esoteric, speculative, and New Age subjects. Our mission is to publish quality books that will make a difference in people's lives without advocating any one particular path or field of study. We value the integrity, originality, and depth of knowledge of our authors.

Our readers are our most important resource, and we appreciate your input, suggestions, and ideas about what you would like to see published.

Visit our website at *www.redwheelweiser.com* to learn about our upcoming books and free downloads, and be sure to go to *www.redwheelweiser.com/newsletter* to sign up for newsletters and exclusive offers.

You can also contact us at *info@rwwbooks.com* or at
RED WHEEL/WEISER, LLC
665 Third Street, Suite 400
San Francisco, CA 94107